Studies in Economic Ethics and Philosophy

Springer
Berlin
Heidelberg
New York
Barcelona
Hong Kong
London
Milan
Paris
Singapore
Tokyo

Studies in Economic Ethics and Philosophy

P. Koslowski (Ed.)
Ethics in Economics, Business, and Economic Policy (out of print)
X, 178 pages. 1992
ISBN 3-540-55359-2

P. Koslowski and Y. Shionoya (Eds.)
The Good and the Economical
Ethical Choices in Economics and Management (out of print)
X, 202 pages. 1993
ISBN 3-540-57339-9

H. De Geer (Ed.)
Business Ethics in Progress?
IX, 124 pages. 1994
ISBN 3-540-57758-0

P. Koslowski (Ed.)
The Theory of Ethical Economy in the Historical School
XI, 343 pages. 1995
ISBN 3-540-59070-6

A. Argandoña (Ed.)
The Ethical Dimension of Financial Institutions and Markets
XI, 263 pages. 1995
ISBN 3-540-59209-1

G.K. Becker (Ed.)
Ethics in Business and Society.
Chinese and Western Perspectives
VIII, 233 pages. 1996
ISBN 3-540-60773-0

P. Koslowski
Ethics of Capitalism and Critique of Sociobiology. Two Essays with a Comment by James M. Buchanan
IX, 142 pages. 1996
ISBN 3-540-61035-9

F. Neil Brady (Ed.)
Ethical Universals in International Business
X, 246 pages. 1996
ISBN 3-540-61588-1

P. Koslowski and A. Føllesdal (Eds.)
Restructuring the Welfare State
Theory and Reform of Social Policy
VIII, 402 pages. 1997
ISBN 3-540-62035-4

G. Erreygers and T. Vandevelde
Is Inheritance Legitimate?
Ethical and Economic Aspects of Wealth Transfers
X, 236 pages. 1997
ISBN 3-540-62725-1

P. Koslowski (Ed.)
Business Ethics in East Central Europe
XII, 151 pages. 1997
ISBN 3-540-63367-X

P. Koslowski (Ed.)
Methodology of the Social Sciences, Ethics, and Economics in the Newer Historical School
From Max Weber and Rickert to Sombart and Rothacker
XII, 565 pages. 1997
ISBN 3-540-63458-4

A. Føllesdal and P. Koslowski (Eds.)
Democracy and the European Union
X, 309 pages. 1998
ISBN 3-540-63457-6

P. Koslowski (Ed.)
The Social Market Economy
Theory and Ethics of the Economic Order
XII, 360 pages. 1998
ISBN 3-540-64043-6

Amitai Etzioni
Essays in Socio-Economics
XII, 182 pages. 1999
ISBN 3-540-64466-0

P. Koslowski (Ed.)
Sociobiology and Bioeconomics
The Theory of Evolution in Biological and Economic Theory
X, 341 pages. 1999
ISBN 3-540-65380-5

Ioanna Kuçuradi (Ed.)

Ethics of the Professions: Medicine, Business, Media, Law

Springer

Prof. Dr. Ioanna Kuçuradi
Hacettepe University
International Federation
of Philosophical Societies
Department of Philosophy
Beytepe 06532
Ankara
Turkey

Editorial Assistant
Nermin Yavlal-Gedik

Printed with the support of the Novartis Foundation
for Sustainable Development

ISBN-13: 978-3-642-64280-7 Springer-Verlag Berlin Heidelberg
New York

Cataloging-in-Publication Data applied for
Die Deutsche Bibliothek – CIP-Einheitsaufnahme
Ethics of the professions medicine, business, media, law: Turkish and German perspectives / Ioanna Kuçuradi (ed.). – Berlin; Heidelberg; New York; Barcelona; Hong Kong; London; Milan; Paris; Singapore; Tokyo: Springer, 1999
(Studies in economic ethics and philosophy)
ISBN-13: 978-3-642-64280-7   e-ISBN-13: 978-3-642-60153-8
DOI: 10.1007/978-3-642-60153-8

Hardcover Design: Erich Kirchner, Heidelberg

SPIN 10546626   42/2202-5 4 3 2 1 0 – Printed on acid-free paper

Preface

The present volume consists of papers presented to a seminar on "Philosophical Ethics and Professional Ethics" organized by the Philosophical Society of Turkey in cooperation with the German Cultural Institute of Ankara, in October 1996.

The topic of the seminar was conceived in the face of the confusion related to the term 'ethics', denoting in certain contexts the relevant field of philosophy and in other contexts sets of norms constituting various professional codes to be respected everywhere during the exercise of a profession.

The aim of the seminar was to discuss ethical problems faced in selected professions, as well as to problematize, from a philosophical view-point, professional ethics in general.

I cordially thank Mr. V. Kage, director of the German Cultural Institute when we started this project, and the subsequent director, Mrs. Marion Hase, as well as her collaborators, for all they have done to help realize the seminar, which adds another ring to the cooperation between the Philosophical Society of Turkey and the German Cultural Institute of Ankara for the international promotion of philosophy —a cooperation which started twenty years ago and has continued uninterruptedly to this day.

I also wish to express my sincere thanks to Prof. Dr. Peter Koslowski, director of the Studies in Economic Ethics and Philosophy, and Prof. Dr. Klaus M. Leisinger, executive director of the Novartis Foundation for Sustainable Development, for making possible the publication of this volume.

Ankara, November 1998 Ioanna Kuçuradi

Contents

CONTENTS

CONTENTS

Philosophical Ethics and Professional Ethics Introduction

IOANNA KUÇURADI

I. On the Different Kinds of "Ethical" Problems

Ethical questions constitute one of the main bundles of questions which philosophy, since its beginning as a field of knowledge, deals with. They are questions directly *related* to the ethical problems we stumble onto, or ignore, in personal and public life, when we take decisions and act. One of the oldest meanings of the term ἤθη (the plural of ἦθος), from which 'ethics' is derived, is 'resort' or 'place where a living being usually takes shelter and lives'.

The questions and problems of ethics as a philosophical discipline, though they are *related* to our decisions and actions in our relations with other persons and with ourselves, are of a *different kind* from the ethical questions and problems we are faced with in life: their ontological and epistemological specificities are different; consequently these two kinds of questions and problems should not be confused, as is usually done. For example, the question "what is right action?" and the question "what is right to do now, in this situation?" do not ask about the same thing. The answer of the former would be the "definition" of 'right action'; while an answer to the latter could be given only by one's finding out what he should or can do in that given-unique situation in which he finds himself, e.g. he could say "I have to resign from this post". As is obvious, this latter answer is no philosophical knowledge. The questions raised *now* in various professional ethics belong to neither of these kinds of questions.

As a matter of fact, though we are faced with ethical problems every moment in life, in the history of philosophy dealing with ethics there have been up-and-downs. Thus in our century, though ethics as a philosophical discipline, under the influence of logical empiricism, remained in the background for a long time, recently —i.e. during the past fifteen or twenty years— we have witnessed an increase in the importance ascribed to "ethics" and a renaissance of ethics, but mainly *outside* philosophy, i.e. we witness an outburst of various professional ethics, as they are called, as well as an increasing mention of the need for a "new ethics" in dealing with global problems. Put very briefly, the word 'ethics' is now *en vogue*.

What are all these endeavors searching for? And how do questions raised in various professional ethics differ from those asked in philosophy and in everyday life?

The ethical questions raised in everyday life are **a**) questions concerning *one given* person's evaluation of *one given* situation, action, person etc. and **b**) questions concerning the attitude that *one given* person —you or me— has to take, or the action(s) he has to perform in *one given* situation. The questions raised in professional ethics on the other hand, concern what one should or should not do *in general*, while practicing the given profession; they are questions concerning ethical and legal norms. Their answers, if given, appear as international declarations, conventions and moral professional codes.

Now, what is the specificity of ethical questions in philosophy? Or: what do they ask about? The answering of the latter question presupposes an exposition of the main approaches in and to ethics in the history of philosophy and today. I shall not do this here, i.e. I shall not present here what *I* see in the history of ethics, neither shall I expose my own approach *in* ethics[1]; rather I shall confine myself to sketching what is widely accepted concerning the questions of ethics and its history. This can help us see how professional ethics developed, as well as explain why today various professional ethics revolve around justifications of norms —and not

1 To be found in my *Etik* [Ethics], Ankara (Philosophical Society of Turkey) 3rd ed. 1996.

infrequently of contradictory norms, a fact which corroborates the widespread acceptance that there is a plurality of "truths".

II. Prevailing Approaches to Philosophical Ethics

According to most of the *textbooks* on ethics, the questions of ethics are built around "the good" —e.g. "what is good?", "what is good life?", "how should one live?", "what are ethical values?" etc.— and around "freedom" —e.g. "is man free?", "what is freedom?", "what man is responsible for?" etc. It escapes attention that each of these questions, or at least those here enumerated, asks about different things. Still, the different answers given to each of these questions have led some philosophers to the acceptance of total relativism, whose latest manifestation is postmodernism; and some others to dealing with the problem of "the scientific (or rational) justification of norms" and its methods. This latter, or the question of the foundation of ethics, as it is often called, constitutes one of the main foci of discussion in present-day ethics.

Thus when we look at what is being done today in the name and under the name of ethics in philosophy, we see *theories* which try to justify existing norms (utilitarism, contractualism), *theories*, which try to introduce meta-norms (Rawls), and *theories* which oppose relativistic ethics, but which still move within the same framework ("communicative ethics", "the ethics of discussion"-*Diskursethik* etc.). But all of these theories —be they normative (deontological) or metaethical, or even attempts to connect them— share the main basic assumption that ethics consists of problems of norms.

As for the *textbooks* on the history of ethics: according to most of them ethics has shown the following line of development: ancient Greek ethics was eudaimonistic ethics (ancient Greek philosophers tried to answer "what should we do or how should we live in order to become happy?"); with Kant starts deontological ethics (i.e. ethics which attempts to bring formal "laws" of universal validity); in the XXth century (with Max Scheler and Nicolai Hartmann) starts axiological ethics; and today the point that ethics has reached is metaethics (i.e. ethics which tries to analyse and justify or found propositions of norms).

According to this picture of ethics —which I personally find highly problematic indeed—, ethics consists of attempts to establish, in the face of the existence of different (conflicting) and changing ethical norms, **a)** definitions of *the* good, as well as "universally" valid norms for action and **b)** metanorms to use as criteria for the evaluation of existing norms and as a basis for their foundation. This is the alternative of normative ethics-metaethics, to which we may add —in order to complete the picture— the attempts to bring them together, like those of William Frankena in the USA[2] and those of "communicative ethics" or "the ethics of discussion" in Europe, which latter concerns *the way* to reach consensus on certain universal (in the sense of "globally valid") norms:

What is necessary to do today is to put in a complementary connection an axiologically universalistic and deontological ethics with a neoaristotelian ethics, which refers to forms of existence. But for this, it is necessary ... that the universalistic-deontological ethics prevail over the ethics of an individual's proper assumption.[3]

This, or something similar, is what the so-called "ethics of discussion" wishes to achieve. This approach to ethics is one of the variants of the theory of the "rational" or "scientific" justification of norms. It concerns *the methods* of reaching a consensus on norms.

Still, in spite of all these theories of —or approaches in or to— ethics we are faced with many ethical questions in life whose answers we are unable to justify sufficiently (of course, so long as we remain within the same framework), or whose contradictory answers are both justified "rationally" or "scientifically", as we see now in the case of some questions of bioethics. This leads some philosophers to speak of many "truths", as I already said, and some others —as E. Tugendhat expresses it— to speak of the "helplessness of philosophers to meet the ethical challenges of our time".

---

2 W. FRANKENA: *Ethics*, Englewood Cliffs/N.J. (Prentice-Hall) 2nd ed. 1973.

3 K.-O. APEL: "Une éthique universaliste est-elle possible?", in: R. KLIBANSKY and D. PEARS (Eds): *La Philosophie en Europe*, Paris (Gallimard/UNESCO) 1993, p. 502.

III. From "Normative Ethics" and "Metaethics" to "Professional Ethics"

How did philosophical ethics arrive at metaethics, which is only one, yet now the most prevailing, approach in ethics? If we can see this, we can also perhaps see how this outburst of various professional ethics came about, as well as see the origin of the difficulties they are now confronted with.

So far as I can see, metaethics —which amounts to reducing ethics to epistemology—, appears to be the result of a concurrence of two different views in philosophy: of the acceptance that ethics is a normative discipline, which developed as I mentioned a few minutes ago, and of the spread of neopositivistic epistemology:

If one *accepts* that the object that ethics deals with, in one way or other, is moral norms —i.e. value judgements and principles of action, etc.—, and then looks at these norms with logical empiricism's criterion of "scientificity", it is true that propositions of norms *do not* show the specificity of the propositions that this trend calls "scientific" —i.e. they are not verifiable or falsifiable *empirically*, in the sense of being verifiable or falsifiable on the basis of sense data. But to put all ethical propositions, including all propositions of ethical norms, under the heading of "metaphysics" presupposes the acceptance of that dichotomic neopositivistic criterion, which is epistemologically a very problematic one, as also the pragmatistic criterion of truth is; because they are "material" criteria, in the technical sense of the term.

This acceptance that ethical norms are not "scientific" has, nevertheless, corroborated the demand that "science" should be "value-free". Still this demand, imposed in a world which does not differentiate between *the knowledge* of ethical value or values and value judgements or ethical norms in general, has created results, which probably were not intended. What the demand that "science" should be "value-free" *in fact* demands, is that scientific research and the application of (scientific) knowledge not be hindered by religious and cultural value judgements and norms. Still this demand has led to eliminating *all kinds* of value questions in scientific research and in the application of the products of various sciences. The idea that for the sake of the progress of science "everything possible may be done", or, "everything is permitted" has gained ground in the scientific community. Thus in different sciences —biology, bio-chemistry, physics, medicine, etc.— everything possible has begun to be attempted without any limits, and the outcome is used without any limitations, by those who wish to use it for any reason; since standard-setting and legal arrangements on such issues follow with great delay, and usually only after the appearance of "intolerable" results.

Thus this "value-free" development of the sciences and of technology, coupled with private or political interests, has led humanity to various impasses, among which we find also certain global problems, as they are called.

This fact on the one hand has paved the way to the revolt against "scientificity" and "rationality" or "western rationality" and to the search for "spiritual values", to be found according to many people only in religions; and led to the acceptance of "many rationalities" and the *cult of cultures* we observe[4]; but on the other hand also has given rise to the search for *common norms*, to be made valid globally.

The parallel of the empirical search for common norms appears in philosophical ethics as attempts to put forward metanorms.

Thus at the origin of the outburst of various professional ethics that we see in the last two decades, the coincidence of this search for common norms *and* of the prevalence of metaethics in philosophy seems to have played the main role.

Though the ethical problems faced in various areas of human endeavor are *in their singularity* totally different, what makes it possible to speak of "professional *ethics*" is that all of them are —each on its own account— seaching for *common* norms, to be *made* valid by the due procedures and be used during the exercise of this or that profession. But it escapes attention that any norm —i.e. whatever its epistemological and axiological specificity might be—, can be *made* valid globally, i.e. become a *common* norm.

4 Cf. I. KUÇURADI: "Modernity as a Concept and as a Project, or 'Modernity', 'Modernization' and Beyond", in: M. WAHBA (Ed.): *Cultures in Conflict or in Dialogue?*, Cairo 1991, pp. 81-97.

IV. Ethical Problems in Some So-called Professional Ethics

Let us now take a look at what historically gave birth to, or contributed to bringing to the fore, the "professional ethics" to be dealt with in this Seminar, since these and other "ethics" are considered to be the way to introduce the ethical concern in those areas —an assumption that causes "professional ethics" to multiply every day.

1. Ethical Problems of "Biomedical Ethics"

What has given birth to bioethics are the reversible or irreversible results of the indiscriminate *use* —by *some* scientists and decision makers— of scientific knowledge. In the face of these results and other anticipated ones, *some other* people —scientists included—, who find them "unethical", think that it is necessary to put limits on the scientifically possible, and expect that "bioethics" or "biomedical ethics" will bring the norms needed for this limitation —norms to be also introduced in the training of scientists in the relevant disciplines. What is expected today from "biomedical ethics", is to answer the question of **a)** *what* a scientist in the relevant areas should and should not do *in general*, while conducting research or exercising the profession, and the question of **b)** *how* he should solve a given problem he is faced with, i.e. what should be his criteria. In other words, what is expected, more or less, from "biomedical ethics" is to discuss old and new problems faced in medicine and all related sciences —problems such as selecting among different therapy alternatives, *in vitro* fertilization and transfer of embryo, euthanasia, organ transplantation, determining the moment of death, to enumerate only a few of them— and then bring "rationally" justified norms for legislation and teaching. Still, in all the work done in order to answer all these questions, no sufficient consideration is given to the very simple but basic question of the "what for" of these scientific human activities.

Now the question I wish to raise here in connection with "biomedical ethics" —and subsequently for all other professional ethics— and submit to discussion is the following: Are the different *—in their singularity* different— ethical problems, which natural scientists and medical doctors are faced with during research or practice, also different *in kind*, from those ethical value problems faced in other areas of human endeavor and in life in general? Or, are they ethical problems of *the same* kind, requiring, however, *also* knowledge of the relevant scientific disciplines, in order to tackle them in a cognitively justifiable way and find out what one should do in a given case?

This is a crucial question, which concerns the future of "biomedical ethics" and the possibility of finding out ways to limit indiscriminate use of the results of scientific knowledge and thus of answering expectations, which make people today promote it.

2. Ethical Problems Related to the Environment and "Business Ethics"

Let us now take a bird's eye view at what gave birth to the so-called "environmental ethics" —a denomination which sounds very problematic to me— and to "business ethics".

"Environmental ethics" is conceived today as a way to fight against environmental problems. Environmental or ecological problems constitute a set of problems that we call today global or world problems. They constitute a category of facts[5] or deadlocks into which mankind was led after the Second World War, without noticing it —in spite of the warning of a few scientists—, until some of them have become only too obvious and urgent.[6] Pollution of the air and of waters due to different reasons; accumulation of wastes; increase of concentration of carbon-dioxide and chlorofluorocarbons in the atmosphere, of nitrogen and sulphur compounds in the troposphere, and the climatic changes they have caused and yet will cause; deforestation-desertification, erosion, soil salination; eating up non-renewable resources;

5 Cf. I. KUÇURADI: "Speech", in: I. KUÇURADI (Ed.): *Philosophy Facing World Problems*, Ankara (Philosophical Society of Turkey) 1988, pp. 7-13.

6 Cf. I. KUÇURADI: "Back to the Question of Goals", in: H. ODERA ORUKA (Ed.): *Philosophy, Humanity and Ecology*, Nairobi (The African Academy of Sciences) 1994, pp. xvi-xx, and I. KUÇURADI, "Ethics and 'Environmental Ethics'", in: K. CURI ET AL (Ed.): *Environmental Ethics*, Istanbul (Boğaziçi University, Institut of Environmental Sciences and UNESCO) 1996, pp. 7-11.

scarcity of energy etc.,[7] are usually enumerated among these problems. There are other problems, which have not yet attracted public attention.

We have become aware of a part of them, after they started jeopardizing human life on the planet, and in the case of some of them, after they started threatening welfare *in the industrialized countries.*

All these environmental problems, though they are not of the same nature, are usually considered to have somehow to do with Man's relationship with nature. It is also a widespread opinion that many environmental problems arose from "indiscriminate technological use of scientific knowledge", as happened in "bioethics", or that they are the outcome of so-called technological development. The anticipated solutions are based on such an assumption or explanation.

Allow me, please, to disagree with this opinion, because such a claim takes into account only one factor which caused these problems, but loses sight of a certain kind of factors, which have caused the *entanglement* of various independent events and facts, which lie at the origin of the situation in which we find ourselves at the end of the century —a situation of which, I am afraid, we sense only some symptoms, while not being sufficiently aware of certain of the factors that caused it. These factors we lose sight of are *our* global decisions, and the actions *we* performed to carry them out.

If we take a look at what has happened in this respect since the end of the Second World War, keeping in mind also such factors, it appears that the deadlocks faced especially, but not only, in industrialized countries, and which alarm us, are due rather than to "technological development" or "indiscriminate technological use of scientific knowledge", to the global decisions *we* took and the actions *we* performed in this respect; i.e. they are due *not* to an indiscriminate but a *voluntary* technological use of scientific knowledge *in view of given objectives* —objectives upon which *we* have decided. To put it plainly, behind these problems we find the so-called "development" —which is still our *idée fixe*— set, after the Second World War, as *the principal* objective of national policies in almost all the countries of the world.

Developmental policies followed in most of the industrialized countries not only opened the way to "indiscriminate technological use of scientific knowledge" but also promoted it, without thinking of its effects on human beings and on nature —even of its easily predictable effects, probable at that

7 Cf. UNESCO Draft Medium-Term Plan (1984-1989), par. 68-86.

time and now a reality. These policies, determined in the industrialized countries by the principle of "the bigger the better" and coupled with political calculations —including the production of all kinds of weapons— have caused these effects —including environmental problems. Are these policies an "indiscriminate" technological use of scientific knowledge or a voluntary and conscious one?

Yet the effects of these policies followed in the industrialized countries have consequences, including environmental ones, for the so-called "countries on the way to industrialization" as well; where, at the origin of the environmental problems they now face, we see another factor besides *their* developmental policies, i.e. this time policies aiming at the increase of *per capita* income, industrialization and development of their technologies. This factor is the unlimited increase of population in these countries.

This increase of population in the "countries on the way to industrialization", coupled with poverty prevailing in most of them, together with *their* developmental policies, caused rapid urbanization with all its special effects we see in many cities in Asia, Africa and Latin America, to which some of the environmental problems faced there are also due, e.g. migration from rural areas to these cities, giving rise to wretched shanty towns and slums. These same factors have also caused the migration from these countries to oil-producing and industrialized countries and the ghettos we see there, with all their environmental problems.

All these are well known facts. Still it escapes attention that some of these facts are *at the origin* of the environmental problems we face and some others are their *outcome*. If we wish to master these problems, we must not confuse them, but treat them differently in our endeavor to find solutions. Neither must we lose sight of the fact that, though the threats are global, the problems faced in these different categories of countries are different —a difference to be kept in mind, in our search for global solutions.

Now in the Fourth Decade of Development (1990-2000) we find ourselves in an environment, in which all of a sudden we realize that this environment itself is threatening human existence on the planet —an environment which we have not intended to create, but which *we* have *nevertheless* created, directly or indirectly, in a comparatively short period of time, because we did not sufficiently scrutinize *epistemologically* and *axiologically* the specificities *of goals and/or objectives* we had decided to set for our national and international policies. Did we do that, with respect to our anticipated solutions? I am afraid not. The latest example of this, is the unconditional global promotion of the "free market".[8]

What is expected today from "environmental ethics" is to tell us —decision makers and laymen, grown-ups and children— what we *should and should not do*, in order that human beings living now, as well as future generations can merely survive, let alone live more healthily. Business ethics has also developed mainly, though not only, with a view to preventing the intensification of environmental problems which threaten life on earth.

There are trends, i.e. various answers given to the question "what should we do?" —from those focusing on common norms and international legislation, those in the way of extending "foreign aid"[9], to those focusing on the individual and expressing the need for a change in attitudes, e.g. what is called today "ethics of co-responsibility" or "macro-ethics".

I shall not dwell on any of these. My colleagues, who will present papers in the relevant sessions of our Seminar, will, I guess, focus on them. I shall confine myself to pointing —on the basis of the brief analysis I have made— at the need for "environmental ethics", and subsequently for business ethics, to focus on ethical value problems connected with activities and decisions which have created the environmental problems we now face, i.e. business and industry in some regions of the world, and in other regions poverty, as well as to focus on the anticipated ways to "eradicate poverty", to use the term of the Copenhagen Summit.[10]

---

8 Cf. I. KUÇURADI: "Economic Disparaties and the Fashionable Linking of Human Rights, Democracy and the Free Market", in: V. CAUCHY (Ed.): *Violance and Human Coexistence*, vol. I, Montréal (Editions Montmorency) 1997, pp. 330-336 or I. KUÇURADI: "Ökonomische Ungleichheiten und die modische Verknüpfung von Menschenrechten, Demokratie und freiem Market", in: K. M. LEISINGER and V. HÖSLE (Eds.): *Enwicklung mit menschlichen Antlitz. Die Dritte und die Erste Welt im Dialog*, München (C. H. Beck) 1995, pp. 218-225; and I. KUÇURADI: "Goals and Traps in the Ways out of the Current Stalemate of Poverty", in: P. MALASKA (Ed.): *Futures Beyond Poverty-Ways and Means out of the Current Stalemate*, Turku-Finland (World Futures Studies Federation) 1997, pp. 89-99.

9 K. TOMASEVSKI: *Development and Human Rights Revisited*, London and New York (Printer Publishers) 1993.

10 World Summit for Social Development, Copenhagen, March 6-12, 1995.

And in connection with this, I shall repeat my question: are the ethical problems related to environmental problems, which are quite different in their singularity, as well as those dealt with in "business ethics", also different *in kind* from those faced in other areas of human endeavor and in life in general?

3. Ethical Problems Related to Journalism

Ethics in journalism is not a new issue. But this issue has become much more complicated, due to the technological possibilities that mass media can afford now, and consequently due to the increasing role they play in the shaping of so-called "public opinion". This is the reason I shall try here only to put a finger on the philosophical problems underlying the ethical problems faced now in journalism.

These problems are, so far as I can see, directly related to the question of the *goals* of journalism and the problem of *right* evaluation.

One of the main —if not the main— goal of journalism is to make it possible for us *to know* what is going on around us and in the world —i.e. to contribute to the exercise of the individual's basic right to shape *his or her own* opinion on what is going on.

The main job of the journalist —in the broad sense— consists in *mediation*: he is expected to make it possible for us to know what we are not able to witness on our own account, but which concerns us, and thus help the public opinion, which is mostly shaped by the psychological effects of various forms of propaganda and advertisement, be as much as possible an *undeceived* public opinion. Thus the job of the journalist involves not only ethical problems, but also problems of philosophical knowledge.

The basic prerequisite of a journalist's carrying out his job in accordance with the goals of journalism is his capacity of making *right* evaluations —mainly right evaluations of events—, so that he can decide which among the innumerable happenings in a country or in the world is or is not "news", i.e. something that the public *must know or which it would be appropriate for the public to know*. For, what else is "news", but that which a journalist and other media organs think, for quite varying reasons, that the public must know or that it would be appropriate for the public to know?

Selecting among the bulk of events a given one and making out of it "news", let alone giving priority to one or the other detail, i.e. *producing* news, is in itself an evaluation, which, in order to be carried out in accordance with its goal, presupposes, among other knowledge, philosophical knowledge, including ethical value knowledge.

When this knowledge —though in itself not sufficient but indispensable for right evaluations— is missing, we are faced with *value ascriptions* and *value imputations* to events, as I call them.[11] In other words, we are faced with evaluations made by looking only at the consequences that an event bears for "us" —for a given group—, i.e. at consequences which are unavoidably different from those the same event bears for another group; or we are faced with the "explanation" of an event from the theoretical view-point or the dogma one believes to be true.

These ways of evaluation make possible the different evaluations or supposed explanations of the same event that we see in life, and which people usually call "evaluations from different view-points", still without differentiating between different views (i.e. opinions) *on* the same issue and different views (i.e. aspects) *of* the same issue.

Ethical questions are involved in the journalist's job in itself; they don't start, as many people think, with the conscious, partial or total manipulation of the camera, with inventing "news", with *photomontage* etc., which are problems created by the person who, among other things, is a journalist and who is using his medium only as a tool for purposes that have nothing to do with journalism.

Thus different value imputations and value ascriptions of journalists to the same events, made consciously or unconsciously, constitute the origin of different and diverging public opinions. Also what lobbies mostly try to do is to spread their own value ascriptions or value imputations to a given issue, intending to shape the relevant public opinion, or to change a value imputation or value ascription for another one.

On the other hand, oppression of the press, censorship of news based not only on value imputations and value ascriptions, *but also* on right evaluations, and trials of journalists, are made by similar evaluations, but this time not of evaluations of events but of news, i.e. of the text written or the image framed by the journalist. Thus in the face of this state of affairs, in

---

11 Cf. I. KUÇURADI: "From Revolt to Philosophy", in: A. MERCIER and M. SVILAR (Eds): *Philosophes critiques d'eux-mêmes/Philosophers on Their Own Work/Philosophische Selbstbetrachtungen*, (Série publiée sous les auspices de la Fédération Internationale des Sociétés de Philosophie, vol. 11) Bern/Frankfurt am Main/Nancy/New York (Peter Lang) 1981, pp. 105-114.

which for example conscious manipulations of the camera are not censored in the name of the "freedom of press", while there is censorship of news describing or showing what *is*, one does not know what to lament first.

And now I wish to ask once again the same question, this time in connection with such and other ethical problems faced by the journalists or in connection with journalism: are those ethical problems different *in kind* from those we see in other areas of human endeavor and in life in general?

4. Ethical Problems in Legislation and the Administration of Public Affairs

Also the issue of ethical problems faced by, or in connection with, those who make and those who apply the laws is not a new one. It is as old as philosophy.

These problems practically concern everyone who has to do, in one way or the other, with legislation —today first of all every member of the parliament— and everyone who applies the laws, i.e. state and public officers, as well as judges; in other words they concern all those who *deduce, enforce and apply norms*. Theoretically they are related to questions concerning the epistemological and axiological specificities of norms, of their deduction and evaluation, as well as to questions concerning the establishment of a connection between a given case and a norm.

Let me here refer only to one question related to legislation, as one typical example of the point where philosophical ethics and law meet. This is the question of the epistemological and axiological specificity of the premises from which are deduced legal norms at every level of generality.

These premises are often group interests of those in power, other times are parochial or cultural norms, and sometimes are principles of the kind we call human rights. I am afraid we are not sufficiently aware of the epistemological differences between cultural norms and human rights, and consequently of their difference in value.

This leads to the enforcement of norms which in practice exclude each other, as a result of which it becomes possible to impair the rights of individuals *by law*. And this is an ethical problem, among many others, to be tackled mainly by philosophers, and also a clue, by following which we can see the role of philosophy in public life.

Still, are the questions of ethics in the legal profession, in politics and in public administration, whoever faces or whoever deals with them, different *in kind* from those faced in other areas of human endeavor? And: Are the ethical problems faced in various professions and other areas of human endeavor related to questions of norms, or questions of norms only? Or, are they questions related to problems of philosophical ethics and the εργον του ανθρωπου (the job of the human being) as Aristotle calls it?

On the answers of these general questions also depends our planning of the ethical education to be done in various areas of professional training and of ethical education in general, as well as our realizing the role that moral codes could play in various professions. For we may *force* people to act according to norms, but not to act ethically. This each of us has to learn on his or her own account.

Part One

Challenges to "Biomedical Ethics"

Chapter 1

Ethics and the Art of Medicine

PETER KOSLOWSKI

Why do we formulate ethical rules for medical actions? Why are medical ethics necessary? Is it no longer sufficient that the doctor is competent and understands his subject and therefore operates *lege artis* or according to the state of the art? Clearly technical rules alone are insufficient for the humane exercise of the art of medicine. The business of doctors is more than just the technically effective carrying out of operations. Also pertaining to it are an enquiry into the patient's suffering, his physical constitution and life situation. Medical activity cannot simply concern itself with technical demands, but must also obey pragmatic imperatives, which require the integration of the business of healing into the situation of the patient's life, the consideration of the effect of the doctor's measures on his happiness in life; and must as well follow the moral imperative, which demands recognition of the patient as a person. [1]

---

1 Cf. P. KOSLOWSKI: "Lebensverlängerung. Nebenwirkungen und Grenzen der ärztlichen Behandlungspflicht aus philosophischer und ökonomischer Sicht", in: P. KOSLOWSKI, PH. KREUZER, R. LÖW (Eds.): *Die Verführung durch das Machbare. Ethische Konflikte in der modernen Medizin und Biologie*, Stuttgart (S. Hirzel) 1983. pp. 83-100. Reprinted in: P. KOSLOWSKI: *Die Ordnung der Wirtschaft. Studien zur Praktischen Philosophie und Politischen Ökonomie*, Tübingen (J.C.B. Mohr [Paul Siebeck]) 1994.

The pragmatic and the moral imperatives both aim in two directions. They require, on the one hand, the full consideration of the effects of the medical treatment on the subject of the operation, that is the patient, while, on the other hand, they frame the charge laid by the doctor on himself to make full consideration of the technical, pragmatic and moral main effect and side effects of his treatment on the patient into the maxim and motivating theme of his treatment. In material objective respects, naturally, these requirements are identical. The doctor has the duty to weigh up carefully all the effects of his treatment and to opt for the best alternative among the possible treatments. Medical treatment can be directly defined by this obligation and this rule. Should a dimension, such as the pragmatic dimension of the consideration of the effects of treatment, be lacking, then the doctor is acting merely as a moralising technician; should the technical dimension be lacking, then he acts as a pragmatic and moral dilettante; when the moral dimension is not there, then he acts as a mere technician and manager of medicine. Medicine, conceived in its entirety as caring for the patient for the sake of healing and helping, would not be achieved where any of the three forms is lacking.

I. Ethics and the Art of the Doctor

In exactly the same way, medical actions have to be determined by medical ethics as well as by the art of medicine, since it is of the essence of the profession of medicine that it be not only a science but also an art. The art of medicine makes use of the medium of science and technology, in order to bring about an effect on a person by means of treatment. The doctor is obliged and wishes to achieve the healing of the sick person, to "restore" him to health. Medical action is a recuperative action carried out on the person with the aim of restoring his health. Of the two types of action, the *praxis* and the *poiesis* —to appropriate Aristotle's distinction—, medical treatment appertains to the *poiesis*. Aristotle contrasted the activity of communication with others as an end in itself, which he called *praxis*, with the production of a work, which he called *poiesis*. Medicine belongs to the *poietic*, productive activities and thus resembles art.

ETHICS AND THE ART OF MEDICINE

According to Aristotle, *poiesis*, i. e. production and manufacture, has its purpose outside the activity itself and achieves its end in the production of the work or product, whereas it is the characteristic of *praxis*, to which all forms of communication with others and forms of political deliberation and activity belong, that, like theory, it carries its purpose within itself. *Theoria* is ultimately an activity which is an end in itself and aims at the contemplation of essence and truth, which likewise carries its purpose within itself. It is thus recognisable that the Greek tradition of philosophy, of which we too bear the strong imprint, assesses theory and *praxis* highly, whereas it undervalues *poiesis*, the manufacture and production. Since theory and *praxis* are ends in themselves, and since what is done for the sake of itself is, according to the Greeks, ranked more highly than that which is done for the sake of something else, a higher ranking is owed to theory and to *praxis* than to the *poiesis*, whose end is outside the activity, such as the *poiesis* of economy, of fine arts and crafts, likewise of the art of medicine. With the irruption of Christianity —and thereby of Judaism too— into the world of antiquity there came about a significant alteration in these value relationships. Since, according to Christianity, Judaism and Islam, God himself is creator, poet and artist of his world, to bring something about becomes an attribute even of the divine. The repercussions on mankind's understanding of himself could not have been greater: production, work, having been the occupation of slaves, become a characteristic of God.

The profession of medicine is affected at its very core by this revaluation of *poiesis* —the profession, which, during and after Antiquity, moves in a two-fold manner, alongside Christianity, into the central position of mankind's realisation of itself. For one thing, man's creative action is seen in a new light, no longer being evaluated as the production of a slave. For another, the action of the doctor on the individual person acquires a new scale of values. For this reason medicine was probably at all times an attendant on Christianity as it spread, and has remained so to this day. The restorative activity of the doctor is directed at the individual, not at the generality. For the Greeks, however, the individual was precisely the one that was without interest. According to Plato and Aristotle, only knowledge of the universal is possible; the individual is "insignificant" and, strictly speaking, not capable of being predicated. In the words of Thomas Aquinas, who stood in the Aristotelian tradition "Individuum est ineffabile". Also, according to the Greek understanding, the individual derives from matter, but not from form and spirit. We are on that account, according to the Platonic concept, only individuals, in that we present the universal essence of humankind in the general matter, particularised as an individual.

With the three great monotheistic religions, Judaism, Christianity and Islam, as well as once again with the great European Romantic movement at the beginning of the 19th Century, this point of view has been overcome. If we were to present merely the general essence of mankind made actual in the universal matter, really we would not be true individuals at all, but only single instances of a universal species. This does not correspond, however, with our perception of ourselves. We are not mere Christmas cookie moulds, which have been pressed into a general dough mixture, matter. Our individuality goes much further, entering right into the spiritual, and thus into the form.

Why do these general metaphysical considerations of man's activities and of the essence of his individuality exist alongside considerations of ethics in the art of medicine? They indicate that medical activity is not primarily theory and science, and that they are aimed at the establishment of health for the *individual.* Technology and the natural sciences deal with the generality, with conformity to laws of nature. According to Karl Popper a law of natural science is valid until a case is found which contradicts it or falsifies it. It is immediately evident that the art of medicine cannot proceed in this manner. If, with a particular patient, the therapy does not have an effect, that does not mean that it is a false one. Indeed the doctor must even be prepared, so it seems, in particular situations to apply a remedy whose validity has not been at all guaranteed, yet which is perhaps effective solely for this one single patient.

If one looks around at human activities which in a similar way treat universal laws in such a *non-doctrinaire* a manner, one is led towards fine arts and the art of statecraft. Art aims at the individual, at the individual work of art as the synthesis of the general and the particular. The work of art is thereby simply marked out by the fact that it does not confine itself to the generality, but takes on the particular and through it depicts the general. The exception disproves the legitimacy of science, but not, however, the rules of art.

In this sense of the constant necessity of the synthesis of the universal and the particular in the individual patient, the profession of medicine is an art and not merely a science. It embodies the synthesis of medicinal science and the art of the doctor. To be sure, medicine today cannot be practised "unscientifically" or indeed dispense with the results and the methods of precise scientific research. It is just as certain, however, that the other danger exists, namely that medicine in the face of unalloyed science forget its feature as an art, forget that it is obliged to yield to what is individual in an unfettered manner —as would have been said at the time of Goethe "in a flash of genius". *Periculum in generalibus.* The danger lurks in the universal or in generalities. The doctrinaire, in whatever guise, —whether in ideological, religious or scientific garb— is always the foe of true perception of the facts that apply in a given situation.

II. Science and the Ethics of the Professions

What have these considerations as to the nature of medical activity to do with ethics? Ethics are the doctrine of right conduct in its widest sense. It assumes therefore that there can also be wrong conduct, that consequently the initiator of an action possesses degrees of freedom in his actions. In order to be able to recognise that areas of activity are ethically relevant, it has to be recognised that activity in them exhibits degrees of freedom. In the development of modernity a tendency is visible of consciously reducing the degrees of freedom in human activity and wishing to conceal them. In this, science very often serves as a means of such a numbing of the moral factor. It is, indeed, the characteristic of good science, that it limits the degrees of freedom and the arbitrariness of men. Recognised truth is compelling. If one falls from a tower, one has no degrees of freedom in respect to the law of gravity, a fact which one notices straightaway. What is downright fascinating in science is that it engenders assertions of laws, which are "compelling", which everybody has to acknowledge.

This scientific approach to the "compelling argument" becomes ambivalent, however, when it is carried over into areas of life, where the compulsion just does not come to the fore, and that is the case in every area of productive action. In two respects productive action is not always compelling: firstly, man is always free either to act in a certain manner or not to so act. Even where there exists a compulsion to act, it is always still possible to act in this or the other way and to forego this or the other alternative. For another thing, human productive action always takes place within and dependent on a context which individualises in the sense already described. However, the manner in which the context of the action is engaged —in the case of the patient, his individuality, surroundings and life history— is not determined by the general laws of science, but is subject to the artistic imagination or the imaginative power of the person who initiates the actions —the doctor.

Attentiveness and imaginative power are the starting point for morals and ethics. Ethics is not something that arises as a supplementary point of view following the scientific analysis —mainly as an element perceived as disturbing. Rather it is the integration of the non-objective, pragmatic, artistic and moral viewpoints into the scientifically founded analysis and choice-making situation of the professional person acting.

The "professions", the higher specialist vocations, are not sciences but applied sciences and, therefore, arts. Of the professional callings, the medical vocation is an art in a particular sense, since its subject, man as a patient is a particularly non-general and non-standardisable object of the action. It is therefore logical, that the "ethics of the professions", the ethics of the professional vocations, have taken medical ethics as their starting point, in order to have this extended to the ethics of the economy and the ethics of engineering and the technical vocations.

With the question about the ethics of the professional callings and technology, we regain an insight which threatened to be lost because of the emphasis put on scientific methodology —namely, the insight that the accomplishments and arts of men can always be applied ambivalently, since they are activities with degrees of freedom, and that there is no automatism of the good. Plato discusses this problem in his *Hippias Minor* dialogue: the person who understands something about a matter, the expert, can do good and evil equally well, whereas the simpleton can only do good badly and the badly. What Plato wants to say by this is something very simple but often overlooked: in all human activity, it depends on the *intentio recta*, on the right intention, namely, on the intention to pursue the good. For him who does not desire the good, knowledge is a danger rather than an opportunity, since with his knowledge he can do evil better than he could without his professional ability. Hence evil becomes yet more evil due to the power of something good in itself, his knowledge.

Professional activity presupposes in a special way the *intentio recta,* the intention for the good, which does not come into being automatically. Science does not spontaneously give rise to the *intentio recta* purely out of itself. There are, on the contrary, cases conceivable of research which is cynical and contemptuous of humanity. Also, correct knowledge does not lead to right act without the will for good. Knowledge does not of itself guarantee that we also do what we have recognised as correct. There are gaps —gaps in motivation— between knowing and doing, between wishing and accomplishing.

The ethics of the professional vocations, hence medical ethics too, not only have to present the descriptive and analytical task to show what the good might be, but must also create the motivation for doing good or at least promoting it. Ethics attempts to close the gaps in motivation which science and technology often have to leave open, because of the nature of knowledge. For science and technology cannot of themselves state what, in the application of their knowledge, the good is. A genuine natural science experiment can lead to the development of a means for healing and at the same time to a murderous toxin, and the difference between the two lies only in the dose, in the quantity, which is, according to Hegel, the most mindless of all the categories. Technology and the natural sciences are neutral with respect to the motives for engendering knowledge and the purposes of knowledge application, while ethics in common with religion will and must lead to the *intentio recta*, to the intention for the good.

III. The Necessity of Medical Ethics

On this account the public too has a legitimate interest in medical ethics being not only taught but actively appropriated by the medical establishment. This public interest in medical ethics is not an artificial moralising with regard to an area sufficiently technically well-ordered in itself; neither is it *moral aggression*, hostility manifested by moralising against the medical establishment, patients thereby cultivating their resentment against doctors. Much more does the need for medical ethics stem from the lasting asymmetry between the doctor's and the patient's, the expert's and the lay person's knowledge. This asymmetry cannot be resolved completely either by the control of the market and its money prices or by the law and the legal control of medical actions. The doctors's actions vis-à-vis the patient are based so to speak indissolubly on the trust the patient has in his or her doctor and on the ethical imperative for the doctor to satisfy this trust even where the law and the economic control inheret in the patient's option of "exit" to another doctor are not effective. There exist situations where neither the fear of legal sanctions nor the economic incentive work to control the doctor, nor indeed does his need to avoid the exit of those ready to pay for medical services.

There exist situations, over and above the problem of the costs of having recourse to the courts, in which there is insufficient economic control based on the economic interests of doctor and patient and where, through their contractual agreement and the supplementation of economic control by legal regulations, it is not at all possible, since evidence of breach of contract, where such is the case, cannot be produced or can be produced only with great difficulty and cost. The two decisive cases of the failure of the legal and the economic sanctions and checks on medical actions must be mentioned here:[2]

1. Unequal Knowledge

When one of the partners to a contract commands superior knowledge concerning a matter of exchange, the other is forced to trust him and to believe that the knowledgeable one employs his knowledge "in good conscience" and does not defraud the less well equipped party[3]. The doctor may not misuse his superior knowledge in order to advise the patient to have an operation that he knows to be unnecessary. The geologist who conducts a minaral survey for an oil corporation has to pass his research results on to his employer in accordance with his work contract and he may not use them in his own interest by buying the oil-field for himself. The transmission and application of knowledge, even of medical knowledge, is an ethical problem, since it does have not to be scrutinised or proved beyond doubt, from the outside by an observer or a court, that the active party had not possessed knowledge or had knowingly applied it wrongly or to the detriment of others. The fact that knowledge can be applied as befits that knowledge can only be established through a relationship that he or she who possesses the knowledge has with himself, through self-responsibility and conscientiousness rather than through external relationships and external

2 Cf. also P. KOSLOWSKI: *Prinzipien der ethischen Ökonomie. Grundlegung der Wirtschaftsethik und der auf die Ökonomie bezogenen Ethik*, Tübingen (J.C.B. Mohr [Paul Siebeck]) 1988, reprint 1993.

3 Cf. R.C.O. MATTHEWS: "Morality, Competition and Efficiency", *The Manchester School of Economics and Social Studies* (1981), p. 294.

controls. The external control or supervision of the conscientious application of knowledge is only able to seize on or punish gross negligence in the utilisation of knowledge, but not to ensure the efficient utilisation of knowledge in day-to-day medical life. The transmission and the conscientious application of one's own knowledge is always an ethical phenomenon.

2. Monopoly of the Acting Person in the Application of the Resources of his Knowledge and Good Will

Every acting person has a monopoly in respect of his knowledge of his own capability for proficiency and, above all, for his preparedness to apply that proficiency; and a monopoly, also, in respect of his good will. No human can compel another human, not even a doctor, to apply his knowledge in the optimum manner, to manifest good will. Whether a party to the matter, say a doctor, uses the resources of his actions, of his capabilities and of his will in the optimum manner and in accordance with the terms of the contract, in respect of the economy and the law, is, in the final analysis, not to be decided from without. This monopoly in the optimal utilisation of the person's own capabilities is particularly efficacious in the doctor-patient relationship, since every such relationship is a matter of an individualised healing- and business-relationship, singular and non-recurring in time and space.

The doctor, from his quasi-monopolistic position as the one consulted and one not to be replaced without cost and pain, now has the opportunity to take unethical advantage and to charge, for example, excessively high fees or to prescribe unnecessarily expensive treatments on the basis of his particular position in regard to the other party to the contract, the patient. The exploitation of the relatively short-term monopoly position of the doctor administrating treatment, without regard to the criteria of fairness, will make it difficult to maintain trust in the medical fraternity and thus will impede the long-term relationship between doctor and patient, although the individual doctor has for the time being no short-term technical and economic interest in creating trust. Only in the long term perspective is he endangering his own position *and* that of his colleagues. A partner to a contract, who draws every short-term advantage from his monopoly-type position, demolishes trust and puts into question the long-term advantages of trust in the profession he belongs to. The doctor's ethics are the means of avoiding the exploitation of the unequal knowledge of doctor and patient and of his unavoidably monopolistic type of position, and a means of the ethical motivation to uphold the ethical rules. Medical ethics are the means of ensuring that the patient's trust in the doctor is justified, that the doctor feels an obligation to obey the rules of his profession and also of ensuring that he makes them into the precepts he follows in his own dealings.

There are four generally recognised rules, which as precepts for medical specialist actions guide and orientate the dealings of the doctor in everyday life and in arriving at decisions in individual cases. These rules are medical precepts of a higher order, which stand between the technical rules and imperatives of his medical art and science on the one hand and, on the other, the most universal norms of human actions such as, say, the categorical imperative of the ability to universalise one's own actions, otherwise known as the Golden Rule. [4]

The first, most general and oldest rule of medical treatment goes thus: *primum non nocere*, above all do no harm! This rule applies to medical matters and to all actions. As early as Hippocrates it is formulated in the 11th chapter of his book on epidemics. The second rule is: *utilis esse,* be useful! The doctor must be of use to the patient with his treatment or intervention. The third rule is: *salus aegroti suprema lex.* The well-being of the sick person is the highest commandment and purpose of medical treatment. And, finally, the fourth rule: *voluntas aegroti conditio salutis aegroti et artis medici.* The will of the sick person is a condition for bringing about his health and for the practice of the art of medicine. No intervention may be undertaken without the patient's basic agreement, not even when they would be of use. Without the agreement of the patient to an intervention the treatment will be less effective than when it is undertaken with his or her consent.

One maxim for medical action, if not indeed, nowadays, the most important, must be that the doctor's dealings with the patient should be of use. This means that he should not just busy himself with the patient but also help him and treat him correctly in accordance with the matter in hand and his status as a patient. Much of the criticism of the activities of doctors and dentists today stems from the patients' feeling that too much is done to them medically, much of it superfluous. On that account, the doctor must

---

4 Cf. LEO KOSLOWSKI (Ed.): *Maximen in der Medizin*, Stuttgart/New York (Schattauer) 1992.

take even greater pains to satisfy the maxim "First of all, be useful!" Being useful and helpful is to be distinguished from merely being busy. One undoubtedly extreme example taken from jurisprudence may illustrate this. The highest Civil Court[5] in its day found a dentist guilty of causing bodily harm in the following case: A woman patient was suffering from violent headaches and attributed these to an inflammation of the roots of her teeth. The medical diagnosis was that a connection between headaches and the state of the teeth was definitely to be excluded. In spite of this well-founded declaration, the patient insisted that all her teeth be extracted. The dentist acceded to her wish in full knowledge of the medical pointlessness of the measure. Later, the patient successfully laid a charge of bodily harm. The consent she had given was null and void.

As this example shows, the doctor can be busy, even with the agreement of the patient, without really helping, if the negative side effects, say, of a diagnostic or therapeutic treatment are greater than is the effect that is really intended. The perhaps even greater damage is to be taken into account here against the intended benefit. It is essential to weigh up benefits and costs, in order to be able to determine the real success of a treatment. The "success" of a therapy can be defined only through the comprehensive accounting of actual yields and costs, not through good intentions and intended effects. Here it is essential that close attention to the totality of the consequences of one's own acts be the starting point for every morality, and hence the starting point for the morality of medical actions. As Herbert Simon, the theoretician on decision-making, points out, it is close attention, not time, really the resource in short supply.

---

5 *Strafgesetzbuch* (German Penal Law) Arts. 233, 233a, 225, 53 (Ineffective agreement to extensive dental extractions. *Neue Juristische Wochenschrift*, 31 [1978], p. 1206). This judgement has, of course, given rise to considerable criticism: cf. H.-L. GÜNTHER: *Strafrechtswidrigkeit und Strafunrechtsausschluß. Zur Rechtswidrigkeit als Straftatmerkmal und zur Funktion der Rechtsfertigungsgründe im Strafrecht,* Köln u.a. (Heymann) 1983, p. 349.

IV. Achievement and Limitation of Rules of Decision-making for Medical Actions in Situations of Uncertainty

Now it is difficult to fulfil the maxim "*primum utilis esse*" —firstly be useful— for two reasons. The doctor acts in general under conditions of uncertainty, or at least where there is risk. Acting where there is uncertainty means that the apportionment of probability of the putative results is not known —as is the case, say, with the purchase of shares—, while acting where there is risk means that the apportionment of probability is known —as in a roulette game.[6] It is mainly the case in extensive medical interventions that instances of risk and uncertainty are mixed.

In seeking to comprehend the decision-making problems of doctors, theories which are not robust, i.e. which do not offer easily applicable rules of decision, are unsuitable. In medical practice, it is impossible to undertake detailed accounting of benefits and probabilities. Rather, normal therapies and normal types of decisions have to be set by the medical specialist disciplines. These normal therapies are also the precondition for all guarantee of quality. The guarantee of quality is impossible without an exact description of the normal therapy and of the indications leading to therapy, since it could not be said what the therapy, whose quality is supposed to be guaranteed, consists of. Quality assurance requires, first of all, the exact penetration of the doctor's decision situation in regard to the decision process, as to whether, when confronted with a certain ailment, he should help, for example, by conserving or replacing a tooth.

It is necessary for the establishment of normal therapies and forms of treatment that the medical specialist discipline concerned make the constitutive decisions about types of therapy and thereby impart structure to the doctor's situation regarding the decision process at the operational level. The doctor dealing with a case makes decisions at the operational level, in that he applies the universal types of treatment or normal therapies to the singular situation and state of affairs of his individual patient after detailed consultation with him or her. The constitutive decisions regarding normal therapies have to be made by the specialist discipline through the

6 Cf., concerning the difference between uncertainty and risk, F. KNIGHT: *Risk, Uncertainty and Profit*, New York (Houghton Mifflin) 1921.

professional association of its specialist experts. The specialist area must set down, in consultation with the health policy specialists and the health insurances, the normal useful therapies and situations for treatments, the so-called *media ordinaria,* the regular means, to define the useful practices and state of the medical art. These constitutive decisions shape, more or less, the constitution of a specialist area, toward which the specialist doctors orientate themselves and which they have to actualise in their individual operational case decisions. Every medical specialist field would have to have at its disposition, in this sense, a constitution regarding typical decisions in which has been thought through exactly the benefits and the risks in connection with these decisions and which has set down model decisions for various kinds of ailment.

These normal decisions form case studies, a case-book to refer to, against which the individual doctor can measure his actions and the quality of his actions; they define the state of the art of medicine. The doctor then has to apply the most general, guiding rules of his medical profession for dealing with people according to the rules of the art of medicine. The generally recognised rules of dealing with people are: "Do not cause harm!" "Be useful within the framework of the contractual obligation to the partner in the contract!" "Follow the will of your contract partner!" For the doctor, as a positive definition of the purpose of his actions there is additionally the requirement to promote the health and well-being of his patient.

The rules for promoting the welfare of the patient and being useful to him require, in concrete situations of sickness and pain, the realisation of the benefit to this particular patient. Therefore, to be of use to the patient is often difficult, since there is uncertainty about the future —uncertainty about how the therapy will work, whether the patient's body will accept it and so forth. Therefore the doctor cannot be *certain* of maximising the benefit, he can only *take a risk* and try to make the *expected* benefit as great as possible. To maximise the expected benefit or expected value means, according to the theory of decision making, to select that alternative whose expected utility, multiplied by the probability that the hoped-for results will occur, is the highest among a given number of treatment options.

An example: If a dentist has two options, either treatment for the conservation of a tooth or an extraction and its replacement by a bridge, so the advantage of keeping the tooth being perhaps 100, the probability that the tooth remains intact is, however, only 20% or 0.2. The bridge has an advantage of 10; the probability that it will last for 10 years is, however,

90% or 0.9. The expectation value of the first alternative is about 100 x 0.2 = 20, while that of the second alternative, extraction, is 10 x 0.9 = 9. According to the rules of expectation value, the first alternative, the conservation treatment, is the one to be selected. This rule is named after its discoverer, the Englishman Thomas Bayes, and is also called the Bayes decision rule. Among all the alternative decisions, the one which promises the highest expected utility should be the one selected.

The rule of maximising the expected utility in the decision requires that the decision maker should grasp that decision, which, *according to its consequences*, commands the highest expected utility. The expected utility is determined as the sum of the products arising from the use and the probability of the appearance of the possible consequences. For the constitutional decisions of a medical association with regard to normal therapies, this complicated procedure is useful, but in everyday practice it is applicable only after it has become a robust rule of thumb.

Of course, it can also easily be shown where the boundaries of relief for the individual lie when coming to a decision through the process itself of finding the decision, following the rules of calculating the expected utility. This process cannot, much as we would wish it, completely relieve the individual of the decision and of the compulsion towards existential commitment in making it.

The selection of alternative decisions using the Bayes decision rule or another calculation of utility and probability, external to the person making the decision, must become relativised insofar as the apportionments of probability are not known in general and, consequently, the person making the decision has to estimate probability according to his subjective evaluation, so that his subjectivity always remains quite substantially involved in the field of play. The *probabilitas interna,* the internal probability, that is the conscientious and deligent evaluation of expected results of treatments and their probabilities, cannot be seperated, in the decision that is ultimetely arrived at, from the *probabilitas externa*, the external probability, given by empirical research and practice of the medical art, the reliance on the external calculation of "objective" probabilities. Neither the internal nor the external probability may be realised alone. The doctor must rely not only on the external data of the Tables of Probability concerning alternative therapies, but must combine these data *and* the accurate examination of the patient, in the assessment of the individual case and his commitment to the individual patient.

We incline towards shifting the burden of decision onto others. The attempt to take from the doctor the burden of decision by means of computerised decision-making procedures and expert systems sorts with our desire to replace the internal decision and weighing up, to replace the *probabilitas interna* with the *probabilitas externa*, with the external calculation of parameters and variables that have been quantified. All decision processes, however, can only be complements to and partial alleviations of the real internally committed decision-making.

The evaluation of the utility of the medical effects and side effects of treatments is not independent of the assessment of the probability that they will appear; they are at the most heuristically separable. A person who has an interest in a particular result will consider it to be probable more than does a person who has no such interest. A moral person has a different view of what is probable than does an immoral person[7]. An ethically orientated, conscientious doctor makes estimates of the probabilities in general in a different way and more carefully than a more thoughtless doctor and operator and arrives at different "external" probabilities.

External probability can never take the place of internal deliberation about the choice of treatments. Pascal has pointed out the significance of integrity in the evaluation of main effects and of unintended side effects. "*Diriger l'intention*" is a means of declaring to be only an unwanted side effect, something that one really wants when following another alleged purpose.[8] One can also "direct" probabilities in that, through wishful thinking, the assumptions about them are so modified, that they suggest the alternative that one in any case prefes. This re-labelling of the real intention to appear as only a side effect being accepted willy-nilly is something to be judged critically, above all where the intention is directed at an effect which must be judged to be bad in itself.

The danger of the *diriger l'intention* exists also for the way in which the decision is made after calculating expected utility. The interests of the doctor and those analysing the decision will not end with the calculation regarding the expected benefits and the array of probabilities of events occurring. His interests will so "direct" his intentions in their own favour, that the

---

7 Thus J. H. NEWMAN: *An Essay in Aid of a Grammar Assent* (1870).

8 B. PASCAL: *Lettres provinciales,* lettre 7, in: B. PASCAL: *Œuvres*, published by L. Brunschvicg and P. Boutroux, Paris (Hachette) 1908, Reprint Vaduz (Kraus) 1965, Vol. 5, p. 85.

(subjective) probabilities of the desired outcomes to be brought about are somewhat higher than those of the undesired effects of treatment. Therefore the doctor has to be wary of assessing more highly the expected utility of therapies which suit him more, which he has a better command of or which bring him a larger fee, than he is when he assesses those therapies which he does not like, does not know so well and are cheaper. What is true of this direction of intentions through interests also requires attention when considering all kinds of expert opinions which are based on estimates of probability.

From the critique of the role which the weighing of outcomes and the probabilistic decision theories, such as Bayes' rule, plays in the judgement about alternative medical actions, it follows that a certain robustness is necessary in the rules governing decision making. The decision concerning the action has to be based on the evaluation of the character of that action and on the intuitive evaluation of the causal consequences of the actions. The unavoidability of the internal integral assessment of the consequences and the ethical comprehensive evaluation of the actions cannot be eliminated by external authorities. This unavoidability of the decision is inherent in the "paradox of choice".[9] This paradox signifies: If it is effective, we cannot know what will be the final effects of the decision resulting from an act of choice. Since the decision will alter the course of the world, we cannot continue to record the current course to date or to extrapolate from it. If, on the contrary, we already precisely know, before our actions, the future course of the world, including the effects our actions will have, it is beyond our influence and our decision as to choice is without significance. We have then no real choice.

The boundaries of decision making calculus, the paradox of choice, and the need for the individual self making the decision to take up position in his mind in regard to the decisions he has to take —all of this shows that the intuitive assessment of a decision-making situation and the decision itself must rest on an inner probability, a *probilitas interna*, on that kind of provisional conviction or *certitudo moralis*,[10] which alone is accessible to

9 On the paradox of choice, cf. G. L. S. SHACKLE: *Imagination and the Nature of Choice,* Edinburgh (Edinburgh University Press) 1979, p. 19.

10 Cf. H. G. VAN LEEUWEN: "Certainty in Seventeenth-Century Thought", in: *Dictionary of the History of Ideas*, ed. by PH. P. WIENER, New York (Scribner's) 1968, Vol. 1, p. 304, S. R. LETWIN: "Certainty since the Seventeenth

finite beings. The knowledge of decision theory is less potent by far than the uncertainty about the future.

Even medical actions have to cope with the problem of having only provisional assurance in regard to actions. Universally acknowledged rules regarding decisions can give structure and afford relief to the doctor's decision, but they cannot remove from the doctor either the conscientious weighing up and the decision making itself or his ethical commitment and moral engagement for the patient and for the usefulness of what he does.

Century", *ibid*, p. 312, and H. THIELICKE: *Theologische Ethik*, Tübingen (J. C. B. Mohr) 1965, p. 88.

Chapter 2

Biomedical Ethics and the Limits of Philosophy

YAMAN ÖRS

I. Introduction

Compared with "Medical Ethics", which first appeared in the title of a book written almost two centuries ago[1], the term "Biomedical Ethics" is relatively recent. Apparently, academic circles began to use the latter following the use of "Bioethics", for the first time as is generally believed, in the title of a book[2] published less than thirty years ago. We shall have time here only for a limited discussion on the semantical relationship between the two terms, just as we shall consider the relation between "Biomedical Ethics" and "Bioethics" rather briefly in our context.

As compared with the first part of the title of my paper, the second is evidently a dynamic expression implying a critical attitude to philosophical activity. And while the first half of my presentation is basically of a descriptive nature, directed mainly to the topic of biomedical ethics in a somewhat informative manner, its second half will be more critically oriented, considering the limits of philosophy, above all, naturally, as regards

1 C.D. LEAKE: *Percival's Medical Ethics*, Baltimore (Williams and Wilkins) 1927.

2 V.R. POTTER: *Bioethics-Bridge to the Future*, Englewood Cliffs, N.J. (Prentice Hall), 1971.

ethics and biomedical ethics. To this end, in the following two sections I shall consider the concept of professional ethics as related to biomedical activity, and then biomedical ethics as a subset of bioethics. Later on, in the fourth and fifth sections, I shall briefly discuss the limits of philosophical activity in its relation to ethics and biomedical ethics respectively. It will be seen, in the course of my hopefully critical discussion, that I would not have been able to write a text with the present title, so far as I can judge, if I had not read a relatively recent book, *Ethics and the Limits of Philosophy*.[3]

I am planning to end this presentation by mentioning certain possible implications regarding the philosophy of values and with a critical conclusion of a general sort as regards philosophical activity as a whole.

II. Biomedicine and Biomedical Ethics

It seems that on certain academic and/or professional occasions, the term "biomedicine" is used in preference to its long established homologue, "medicine". This is apparently because certain academicians and professionals would like to stress the multidimensional and complex nature of today's medical activity, with biology gaining an increasingly significant role in contemporary medical ("biomedical") research, notably in the fields of oncology and genetics. Considering the limited space on the present occasion, I shall not be concerned here with unnecessary etymological analyses, and shall use the two terms reciprocally and as semantical equivalents in this context.

As must certainly be the case with other main human activities, the overall conception of medicine has changed in the course of its evolution in accordance with the dominant outlook of the time on the part of both professionals and the public. Today, leaving aside the philosophical and ideological considerations as regards contemporary medical activity, such as a "positivistic" approach to the patient on the one hand and the "anti-psychiatry" movement on the other, the general and established tendency in

3 B. WILLIAMS: *Ethics and the Limits of Philosophy*, Cambridge, Mass. (Harvard University Press) 1985.

medicine seems to be the following: Under the impact of the ever more strongly felt super-economic right politics in the so-called new world order as an external factor, the medicine of our time has as a rule been equated with clinical or diagnostic-therapeutic activity. In conformity with the highly individualistic consumption ideology characteristic of this kind of economic policy, therapeutic means of the present-day medicine —drugs, diagnostic tools, surgical instruments, private hospital buildings, equipment of all sorts...— are used in increasing quantities[4]. Likewise, it may perhaps be safe to say that research in biomedicine has been mainly directed in our time to the development of diagnostic and therapeutic tools. This has evidently been at the expense of public health as an application and community medicine as an overall approach to medical activity. Needless to say, and as one might expect, all this has been reflected in medical education as well, with a great emphasis on the production of physician-technicians and surgeon-heroes[5], possibly in a great majority of medical schools throughout the world.

The situation in *Biomedical Ethics, which deals with moral problems that arise in biomedicine or biomedical activity*, appears to be somewhat different, although perhaps not markedly so. In any case, the physician-patient relationship appears to be very much influenced by the scientific and/or technological advance in clinical medicine. Progress in basic medical sciences and in those branches of science which have a relevance to medicine, such as different branches of biology, also have contributed to the creation of moral problems concerning biomedical ethics. In different aspects of preventive medicine as well, we have witnessed the rise of moral problems. In all these three basic divisions of medicine, the impact of external, that is socio-political, factors appears to have been great, in the past three decades or so, in the shaping of biomedical problems and in the solutions offered for these.

A glance at the contents of a book on biomedical ethics would give us an idea about the range or dimensions of basic problems in this area: the physician-patient relationship and paternalism; truth-telling; informed consent; patients 'rights and the obligations of professionals; privacy and confidentiality; ethical issues in human experimentation; children and prisoners as research subjects; health, disease and values; behavior control;

---

4 Y. ÖRS: "Therapeutic Medicine Globalised" (Letter), *Bulletin of Medical Ethics*, No. 96, (March, 1994), p. 2.

5 *Ibid.*

ethical and conceptual issues; suicide and the refusal of lifesaving treatment; euthanasia; passive euthanasia and the definition of death; the morality of abortion; fetal research; genetics, human reproduction, and the limits of scientific research; social justice and health care, etc.[6]

One may point out at the end of this section that some of the issues just enumerated, such as "social justice and health care", may be collected under the term of "health ethics" rather than "biomedical or medical ethics", but which may in any case be included within the realm of bioethics. Secondly, a moral issue with nonhuman beings as its objects, such as the use of animals in (bio)medical research, might or might not be considered within the scope of biomedical ethics depending on the definitional limits of the latter. Personally, I would consider it a biomedical issue, even if one does not directly refer to the definitional point that biomedical ethics is part of bioethics, as we shall see now.

III. Biomedical Ethics as a Subset of Bioethics

The first book on *Bioethics* was written by V. R. Potter, with the subtitle: Bridge to the Future. The author dedicated his book to the memory of A. Leopold, "who anticipated the extension of ethics to Bioethics". In his historically (and evolutionarily) oriented book, he says that the first ethics dealt with the relation between individuals, and later accretions with the relation between the individual and society. But land still being property, there is as yet no ethic dealing with man's relation to it, and to the animals and plants which grow upon it. As the land-relation is strictly economic, it entails privileges but not obligations[7]. We are in great need of a Land Ethic, a Wildlife Ethic, a Population Ethic, a Consumption Ethic, and an International Ethic, all of which involve Bioethics[8].

6 T.A. MAPPES and J.S. ZEMBATY: *Biomedical Ethics*, New York (Mc-Graw Hill) 1981.
7 V.R. POTTER: *op. cit.*, p. v.
8 *Ibid.*, pp. vii-viii.

Since this book was published more than twenty-five years ago, the term "bioethics" has come to mean different things to different users and/or on different occasions. In its two most comprehensive senses, it means, on the one hand, *environmental or ecological ethics* and *ethics of the professions* on the other. In a somewhat narrower sense, it is the study, mainly philosophical, of *our moral responsibilities towards animals we exploit* for economic, research or other purposes. More relevantly in the present context, it is also an equivalent to Medical or Biomedical *Ethics* with their differing semantical limits, as the case may be[9]. As has been emphasized by the two editors in the first issue of an international journal on *Bioethics*, this field is an interdisciplinary area[10] with contributions from philosophy, medicine and other health professions, law, sociology, education, and so on[11]. These philosophers did not wish to restrict their journal to a narrowly philosophical conception of bioethics.

IV. "Ethics and the Limits of Philosophy"

Leaving a critical though short consideration of the unusual dynamism reflected in the second part of this section's title to the *Implications and Conclusion* section, I may simply give here a rather descriptive account of Bernard Williams' book with the above title. In its Preface, the author points to the fact that according to some broad specification the philosophy of his book can no doubt be called "analytical", together with much of the recent philosophy it discusses. He points out that, compared with other kinds of moral philosophy, "there is no distinctive subject matter of analytical moral philosophy", its distinctive feature being "a certain way of going on, which

9 Y. ÖRS: "Biopolitics in the Light of Bioethics", in: A.V. ARVANITIS and R. KELE (Eds.): *Proceedings of the 5th B. I. O. International Conference held in Istanbul, May 1992*, Athens (Biopolitics International Organisation) 1993, pp. 69-75.

10 H. KUHSE and P. SINGER: "Bioethics: What? And Why?", *Bioethics*, 1, No. 1 (1987), pp. iii-v.

11 H. KUHSE and P. SINGER (Eds): *Bioethics*, leaflet/Oxford/New York (Basic Blackwell) 1988.

involves argument, distinctions, and... moderately plain speech". And as an alternative to the latter, "it distinguishes sharply between obscurity and technicality". He adds later on that he does care that his work should be what he calls "clear"[12].

The ten chapters of Williams's work are as follows: Socrates' question; The Archimedean Point; Foundations: Well- Being; Foundations: Practical Reason; Styles of Ethical Theory; Theory and Prejudice; The Linguistic Turn; Knowledge, Science, Convergence; Relativism and Reflection; and, lastly, Morality, the Peculiar Institution. In the next section, I shall simply make a critical mention of certain points discussed by Williams in some of these chapters. What I intend to consider very briefly in the present section is the points of interest to me in "Knowledge, Science, Convergence"[13]. As an apparently original consideration, the author discusses the end of disagreement in ethics and in science in the light of what he calls "convergence". In his attempt to explain the term in this context, he contrasts the ethical and the scientific because, in his view, the fundamental difference lies between them as two ends of the contrast[14]. Williams remarks that the convergence in his project is one of practical reason, whereby "people came to lead the best kind of life and to have the desires that belonged to that life"; and that "convergence in ethical belief would largely be a part and consequence of that process". "One very general ethical belief would, indeed, be an object of knowledge at that level."[15] Further, "between the two extremes of the one very general proposition and the many concrete ones, other ethical beliefs would be true only in the oblique sense that they were the beliefs that would help us to find our way around in a social world which (his "optimistic program") was shown to be the best social world for human beings". But "there would be a radical difference between ethics and science, even if ethics were objective in the only way in which it intelligibly could be. However, this does not mean that there is a clear distinction between (any) fact and (any) value; nor does it mean that there is no ethical knowledge"[16].

12 WILLIAMS: *op. cit.*, pp. vii-viii.
13 *Ibid.*, pp. 132-155.
14 *Ibid.*, p. 135.
15 *Ibid.*, p. 154.
16 *Ibid.*, p. 155.

This could bring us to a short critical consideration of Williams' views as quoted or mentioned in the above passages.

V. The Limits of Philosophy in Biomedical Ethics

In my view, and as a matter of principle, the limits of philosophy in the case of ethics and, by extension, biomedical ethics should be narrower than the scope drawn by Williams. For one thing, one should clearly see the rather sharp methodological distinction between philosophical approaches to moral problems, both in biomedicine and generally, and the activity of social or human sciences as regards our moral values. In the latter, represented above all by sociology, psychology, and social psychology, the aim is the production, in the light of theoretical approaches, of systematic knowledge as regards human attitudes and conduct. This involves, certainly, an explanation by means of the possible/actual determinants in question such as genetical, psychosexual, socioeconomic, cultural and other factors. And whatever different views there may be regarding "objectivity" in scientific activity in general, the question of "objectivity" in human sciences on the part of researchers (who are at the same time "subjects") must not be confused with the essentially subjective, prescriptive, nature of our values as the subject matter of ethics[17].

On the other hand, philosophical inquiry into our values involves, in the present author's own understanding, a critical semantical-logical analysis of moral utterances[18]. However, this would be different from the "cool" and "distanced" attitude to our moral values, as in the case of the related activity of (typical) analytical (and mostly) Anglo-Saxon philosophers[19]. In my view, *both a rationally analytical and descriptive-evaluative approach to moral problems and a self-analysis and self-awareness of one's psychology and moral thinking in terms of valuation are necessary in moral philosophy.*

17 Y. ÖRS: "Teaching Medical Ethics in the Subjunctive Mood", *Bulletin of Medical Ethics*, No. 93 (November 1993), pp. 31-36.

18 *Ibid.*

19 *Ibid.*

Even in the logical study of our own and others' moral values and value judgements, as in deontic logic for instance, I doubt if, as moral agents, philosophers can totally dispense with the ethical content of their own and other individuals' conceptual/linguistic formulations.

In comparison with ethics in general, biomedical ethics as the study of moral issues taking place in biomedicine offers still different and more differentiated moral aspects, from the viewpoint of both science and philosophy. For all its social, psychological and deeply ethical aspects, medicine/biomedicine is certainly a technical activity, with science, methodologically and academically speaking, as its necessary condition. As one should add in the same direction I think, however bound up it may be with the daily, social life, medical activity has rather different levels of technicality involving quite a comprehensive range of academic/scientific procedures —from biophysics and molecular pathology at the basic science level to micro-surgery or brain scanning as applied medical fields. So far as the content, concepts, language, methods/techniques and other basic aspects of the various medical disciplines are concerned, this high and rich technical aspect of medicine must always be taken into account in the consideration of the related biomedical issues, just because, as might be expected, they are interdependent.

Historically speaking, medical ethics as a body of rules of professional conduct appears to be one of the first, possibly the very first, ethics of a profession, dating back to the time of the third Dynasty in Egypt, almost five thousand years ago. Its problems, like its constitutive elements, have certainly differed from society to society, in the course of time, under the impact of scientific progress and technical development, the developmental level of medicine, philosophical views, belief systems, and so on. I think we may safely say that such "thinking" physicians as Imhotep (at the time of the Third Dynasty), Hippocrates (in Antiquity), Avicenna (as a philosopher-physician in the 11th century Islamic World), Thomas Percival (in 18th-century Europe), and many others in different societies to be sure, have always stressed the concrete human being as the focus of moral guidance in the practice of medicine. This is certainly in sharp contrast to the established "universal" approach of moral philosophers to ethical problems.

With the rise of biomedical ethics in our time, we witness *an increasing interaction between medical ethics and moral philosophy*. The result appears to be a compromise in biomedical ethics, as it were, between the traditionally professional rules of conduct in medicine and the comprehensive ethical principles of traditional (mostly speculative, rationalistic) philosophy. In biomedical ethics today, and as must generally be known in the related academic/professional circles, the two main competing approaches in moral philosophy are the categorical imperative of Immanuel Kant on the one hand, and the utilitarianism of Jeremy Bentham and John Stuart Mill on the other. There have existed, certainly, other views in the evolution of moral philosophy with more or less different approaches to ethical/moral problems in general, and which, too, are now under consideration so far as their applicability to current moral issues in biomedicine is considered. Even when we leave aside the quite unrealistic expectations of moral philosophers regarding the universal acceptance of their moral approaches and/or views, none of their "systems of ethics" appears to be applicable in an overall manner in the case of biomedical activity in its various aspects. One might simply indicate in the present context that the Kantian principles, under the recent terminology of "respect for life", are rather convenient in clinical ethics where patients must be at the very center of the physician's ethical concern *as ends in themselves*; and that utilitarianism is more suitable in medical research, on human subjects for instance, where human beings as volunteers are *essentially a means for the production of scientific generalizations.*

The above considerations, with their direct and/or indirect reference to the limits of philosophy in ethics and biomedical ethics, can now be discussed in a more general and critical way.

VI. Implications and a Critical Conclusion

One might possibly begin this concluding section with a discussion on the use of the term "theory" in philosophy. For all his critical attitude to the limits of philosophical activity in the case of ethics, Bernard Williams also uses this term in the context of moral philosophy, as can readily be seen in the contents of his work mentioned above. This is due to his acceptance, it seems, of the established usage of the term "theory" in philosophical contexts. In its first and foremost, and specific sense, *a theory is a conceptual structure* having certain basic propositions/presuppositions as regards a certain complex set of phenomena in the empirical world. "Theory" is thus a term, *a technical word, which belongs, above all, to the language of science.* My objection as to the use of this term in philosophical activity would seemingly be met by saying that no term, no word for that matter, can be in monopoly of any human activity, and that it can have different senses within the context of differing activities. Such a counter objection, so to speak, would certainly be justified as a matter of principle. However, judging by what those philosophers (and others) who use the term "theory" in a technically philosophical sense may have in mind, the answer to my observation is definitely not so simple. Because the term "theory" is used in a confusing manner in philosophy in that what is meant by it is evidently an alleged (empirically) explanatory function quite similar to, if not identical with, its meaning in science.

We may justifiably say that what appeals most to the philosophers of science and other philosophers interested in scientific activity is the topic of theories (as well as scientific explanation). This is quite understandable because the latter constitute as a rule a set of concepts with an essentially broad scope, comparable to those which are the basic tools of philosophers, that is, concepts of apparently universal content, and any concept, in principle, is abstract —a quality which is eminently appealing to philosophically minded individuals and, certainly, to philosophers. Now, I would like to draw the reader's attention to the specification or proviso mentioned above as regards the term "theory", namely, "in its first and foremost sense". The present context is one of those occasions which would strongly suggest the understanding of the classically minded philosopher as to the relationship between science and his own activity. *The explanatory function of scientific theories* becomes meaningful only to the extent that they lead the way to scientific research and generalizations (with their qualities of confirmation and falsification) on the world of phenomena. Can we say, with any justification, that this is also true in the case of the so-called philosophical theories, whether "metaphysical", "ontological", or "epistemological"? And in the sphere of morality and ethics, where what is called "an ethical theory" is nothing but the sum total of a given philosopher's moral principles and concerns on the one hand, and/or his metaethical approaches or views on the other?

In short, a conceptual framework in the sphere of morality could justifiably be called a theory only with reference to the related social or human sciences. In this sense, and although it has been formulated by a philosopher, a Marxist theory of moral values would be called a theory just because it has been based, to whatever extent, on both direct and historical observation, and irrespective of whether it could be supported by experimentation.

I think the main reason for this state of affairs on the part of traditional philosophers with their rationalistic-speculative endeavour is that they have not been able to see the basic methodological problem of philosophy in our time. As has been put forward by the Vienna Circle, more comprehensively by the logical empiricists of Berlin at the time and, most systematically, by Hans Reichenbach, philosophy can no longer be an activity with its alleged production of "philosophical knowledge" about the empirical world, a function which has totally been assumed or taken over, methodologically speaking, by science. A basic corollary of this revolutionary approach to philosophy and science would be that they must be seen not as rival but complementary activities in man's quest for an understanding and explanation of the world. *The approach and method of philosophy being on the whole conceptually analytical and critically logical, its function in this quest is rather indirect* as compared with the more or less direct involvement of science in the realization of their common purpose. The ultimate (but certainly not absolute) result of the latter activity, scientific knowledge, could possibly be regarded as an end-product, though of course not final product, brought about by a systematic, interrelated body of propositions. It may also be seen, from a more comprehensive and perhaps evolutionary point of view, as part, a distinctive part, of man's overall relationship with the world.

Seen in such a basic methodological perspective, and in spite of the complementarity of the two activities, *science has now become one of the external factors with a limiting function on philosophy* —their historical togetherness based on an assumed, almost overall methodological resemblance no longer exists, in spite of all the efforts of traditionally minded philosophers all over the world. A consideration of the other and "truly" external, mostly social factors with a negative impact on philosophical activity, such as a poor intellectual atmosphere and/or a highly didactic, uncritical education in a given society, would understandably be outside the scope of this paper.

For a detailed discussion on philosophy's, or perhaps rather philosphers', own limiting effect on philosophical activity, one would obviously need much more time. In our topical context, namely ethics, and biomedical ethics as its extension into the medical area, I might just indicate a last point. Such terms as "ethicist", "bioethicist"[20] and "biomedical ethicist", with their unfortunate suffix "-ist", and implying, though not necessarily, an academic and/or professional "authority", strongly suggest the function of a moralist. —a function whereby the latter would "know" the best choice, decision, and line of action so far as human values are concerned[21], and one which is itself doubtful from an ethical point of view.

Irrespective of whether philosophical activity *per se* is a profession or not, and evidently in my view, philosophers as academic people should critically question what they do. And from a moral point of view, this could be justifiably achieved in the light of an ethics of philozophizing[22]. As in the case of any comparably comprehensive human endeavour, such as basic science or the so-called applied sciences (medicine for instance), philosophers, too, would thus be responsible for what they are in the habit of doing in the course of their activity.

---

20 Y. ÖRS: "More on Bioethics Method" (Letter), *Bulletin of Medical Ethics*, No. 111, (September, 1995), p.2.

21 *Ibid.*

22 Y. ÖRS: "The Irresistible Rise of Scientific Philosophy - Philosophism and the Ethics of Philosophizing", *Synthesis Philosophica*, 22, (1996), pp. 447-460.

Part Two

"Environmental Ethics" or "Business Ethics"?

Chapter 3

Environmental Ethics: A New Dimension in Professional Ethics

KRITON CURI

I. Introduction

There are many definitions of ethics. Although the wording may be different, the main idea is always the same: *Don't do to others what you do not want to be done to you.* In other words, ethics, if it is not based on a dogma, is "relative", although the aim is always the same: to adjust and even direct the relations between individuals, between human beings. Ethics is mainly an *anthropocentric concept. Environmental Ethics,* however, differs from the this anthropocentric ethics. It does not aim at adjusting the relations between *two parties*, which can express their opinion and even fight —successfully or unsuccessfully— for their rights. Environmental ethics tries to regulate the relations among *living human beings, nature* —which neither can express itself in an understandable way, nor fight for its rights— and *future generations* which do not yet even exist. In other words, in order to develop properly the concept of environmental ethics, living human beings should be totally liberated from their *ego*, they should stop believing that they are the "*masters of the universe*", they should stop acting in an anthropocentric way, they should consider and respect the rights of all parts

—even of the silent and not existing ones. This is difficult, but it becomes more difficult due to the ignorance, or lack of knowledge, which exists today among humans on environmental issues. Sensitivity is not enough. It is not possible to make right decisions for something which you don't know. Ethics today should not be considered as a "state of mind", it should control actions.

In the environmental field —as in any other field— action should be the result of *knowledge* followed by *concern*. Lack of knowledge or concern leads to environmental tragedies. The birth of environmental ethics is in fact the result of the concern of human beings for their own survival. The present situation of the environment, the exploitation, depletion or degradation of natural resources, climatological changes, deforestation and the extinction of existing species have forced human beings to think more seriously about the environment. As a result of this it has been considered necessary to start developing a code of ethics related to the environment. Is this code objective? It is difficult to say so. There is no doubt that the criteria are again of anthropocentric character and serve mainly the human race. Although, for example, the extinction of any species is considered environmentally unethical, nobody has any objection to the extinction of the microorganisms causing small pox, and everybody applauds the efforts made for the extinction of the AIDS-causing virus. *Are these species too to be preserved*? Therefore statements such as

> There is an emerging consensus, however, that other species have a right to exist, and that the preservation of all species is important not only because they are beneficial to us, but because each species is a part of the integrated, global ecosystem. Species extinction will no longer be tolerated at the cost of progress. We are more likely to see projects being delayed, modified or cancelled entirely to protect one or more species, despite considerable political controversy ... (Drucker, 1994)

are not entirely correct or sincere.

There are still many ambiguities related to ethical problems in environmental issues. The law of nature stating that "*the big fish eats the small one*" is well known, but misinterpreted. In nature, a creature never eats more than is needed for its survival, but human beings do not act in the same way. The "big" and "powerful" of the world believe that they have the freedom to exploit —to "eat" like the big fish— the underdeveloped and developing countries, the poor of the community, etc. —the small fish. And they are never satisfied. Thus the law of nature leads to unethical actions and creates a situation, in which one part of the population exploits the other from an environmental point of view, either on a local or global scale.

Many unethical actions in connection with the environment are performed by people who talk about "ethics and environmentalism". For example, although in the *Universal Declaration of Human Rights* it is mentioned that all human beings are equal, and although the laws of all democratic countries have similar statements, it is an unpleasant fact that many "dirty activities" like the construction of dumping sites or other disposal facilities are never located near the district where the wealthy or powerful of a community live, even if, from a technical point of view, this district may be the most appropriate one in the city. This may be considered as an example of environmental exploitation of one group of people, or lack of *environmental equity*, on a local scale.

All these and other problems of environmental ethics can be dealt with in connection with national and international policies, professional practices and individual conduct.

II. Problems Related to National and International Policies

Policies, programmes and actions of governments according to the principles of environmental ethics should avoid any action which is detrimental to the environment. However, this is not realized either on national or international levels. Some of these actions of international character which are contrary not only to principles, but also to ethics in general, are summarised below:

1. Unequal Use of Natural Resources

As is well known, approximately eighty percent of the total energy produced is consumed by only twenty percent of the world population.

Consequently, a very small part of the population of the world contributes to the pollution caused by energy production. This pollution, however, affects the whole globe, all living creatures. The green-house effect and ozone depletion affect not only those who contribute to their creation, and they affect everybody.

2. Legal or Illegal Exportation of Hazardous Wastes

Hazardous wastes are among the substances which are not desired to be located on or near anybody's property due to the serious detrimental effects which they may have to human health, etc. Because of this, attempts to dump these wastes on some other's land become common practice. The famous NIMBY (not in my backyard) syndrome, which is an invention of the economically developed countries of the world, is a good example of this tendency. The export of hazardous wastes is accoplished in different legal or illegal —but always unethical— ways. Some of these ways are "bribing of the administrators" of undemocratic underdeveloped countries; false statement about the quality of the product; playing around with the definition of "hazardous wastes" etc. An example of these unethical ways is the export of the ash generated from the Philadelphia incinerator to Haiti as fertilizer and to Guinea as construction material! It is true that some attempts have been made to stop this catastrophic traffic. One example of this is the Basel Convention, accepted on 22.03.1989. Some environmentalists claim that this Convention was a serious attempt to stop the export of hazardous wastes. Others, however, claim that this Convention "legalized illegal action".

3. Export of Dirty Industries

Another problem faced in this is the export of *dirty industries*. Multinational companies taking advantage either of the unfavourable economic situation, or the lack of proper legislation and control, in economically underdeveloped and developing countries, dump the hazardous wastes produced by factories there, claiming many times that they do this in order to contribute to the development of the country concerned. Thus, although they benefit in every way by the products of these industries, they leave their wastes in another country, thus causing problems to innocent people who have minimal benefit from this industry.

4. Donations and Gifts of Bad Intention

There are cases in which hazardous wastes are exported to economically developing countries under the name of "*aid*", "*donation*" or "*gift*". An example of such attempts was a proposal made by a German company to build a road along the coast of the city of Bandırma in Turkey, as a "gift". Investigations have shown that they were planning to use, instead of sand or aggregate, the ash from the hazardous waste incineration plants of Germany.

III. Problems Related to Professional Practices

Principles of environmental ethics should be included within the code of practice of any profession, if we consider that the main aim of all professions is to contribute to the overall long-term good or happiness of the world and of all its inhabitants. It is interesting, however, to notice that the concept of environmental ethics is relative and varies from profession to profession. For example, although a military officer considers the destruction of a forest, if needed, an entirely ethical action, the opinion of an ecologist is entirely different.

The concept of environmental protection is often used and misused for the promotion of certain products. For example, replacement of wood by another product is often presented as "environmentally friendly action aiming at the protection of forests". However, it is well known that wood may be used without causing detrimental effects to the environment provided that forest industry is developed properly.

Similarly, ecolabelling is often misused in order to maximize profit.

From the engineering point of view, the selection of clean or non-waste technologies is a "must", if the rules of environmental ethics are to be obeyed, but this is rarely done due to ignorance or to other reasons.

Decision-makers such as politicians, although in the pre-election period they preach about the environment and environmental ethics, often change their attitudes after they come to power, and in the end take decisions which have detrimental effects for the environment.

IV. Problems Related to Individual Conduct

Recently people have started being more concerned with environmental problems in everyday life. They have started preferring "environmentally friendly products". Efforts to preserve certain endangered species have started becoming more systematic, often leading to positive results. People have started publicly criticizing practices detrimental to the environment. However, awareness and sensibility in this respects are still not at the desired level.

V. Conclusion

Although considerable advances have been made in spreading environmental ethics, the syndrome of "double —or even multi— standards" continues to prevail. Crucial ethical problems exist in the decisions and actions of those governing the world.

Our educational system is not adequate for developing sensitivity to and responsibility for environmental issues. To improve this situation, the following can be recommended:

a) Proper systematic education should be encouraged by all means, because "right action" depends on knowledge and concern. The concept of environmental ethics is not an easy one, because runs counter to the egocentric character of human beings. Protection of the rights of others —especially of those who can not express themselves— needs additional efforts. It should be always remembered that the human race is not "*the master*" or "*the owner*" of the environment, but simply the "*care-taker*" of the universe to which it also belongs.

b) Codes of ethics for industry, the government, the media and the public should be prepared and continuously developed.

c) Economical sanctions should be applied to those who do not respect the principles of environmental ethics. For example, no credit should be given by banks to those destroying the environment.

d) Putting an end to double standards should be a goal of environmental activities. The sensitivity which is shown when an industry is established in a developed country should be also shown when it is established in a developing country. Products which are not permitted to be used in the country of origin, should not be permitted to be exported to other countries either.

Environmental ethicism should stop being a means of "image building". It should be sincere, objective and consistent.

References

CURI, K.: "Environmental Exploitation and Environmental Ethics", in: CURI, K., DOUGLAS, I., GHAZNAWI, A., İŞLİ, İ. (Eds.), *Environmental Ethics*, Istanbul (Boğaziçi University Press) 1996.

DRUCKER, M. P.: "Ethical Responsibilities of Environmental Engineers", 1994.

FERGUSON, R. G.: "Environmental Ethics in Canada", in: CURI K., DOUGLAS, I., GHAZNAWI, A., İŞLİ, İ. (Eds.), *Environmental Ethics*, Istanbul (Boğaziçi University Press) 1996.

KOCASOY, G.: "Environmental Ethics and Eco-labelling" in: CURI, K., DOUGLAS, I., GHAZNAWI, A., İŞLİ, İ. (Eds.), *Environmental Ethics*, Istanbul (Boğaziçi University Press) 1996.

Chapter 4

Business Ethics, Multinational Corporations and Developing Countries

KLAUS M. LEISINGER

I. Introduction

Questions about the ethical justification of men's dealings have kept philosophers busy throughout the ages. Whether you now refer to Laotse, Confucius, the compilers of the Biblical evangelical texts or the Fathers of the Church, Augustine or Thomas Aquinas, they all have comparable ideas of right and wrong human behaviour as well as of meaningful human existence.

Those among us who are really interested in the principles guiding actions can draw on Immanuel Kant, Max Weber or Hans Jonas for advice.

To reflect philosophically on ethics is, without doubt, a fulfilling and spiritually demanding concern. If one wants to do more, however, than bring the traditional perceptions of moral philosophy to men, or even to preach romantic idealism to them, then ethics —also business ethics— must "be hauled down from the heaven of 'ideas' or 'values' and placed into the reality of everyday life." To act in a responsible manner does not mean here to act with a superior moral obligation in mind, but "out of a real world relationship, in which one really has to account for his dealings in a relationship of dialogue".[1] *Real* persons, with all their strengths and weaknesses, have to be taken as the basis of such a discussion, not *ideal* ones, such as we would all prefer but scarcely ever meet.

The aim of the economy is to cover the needs of everyone and to achieve this it requires a sensibly ordered interplay of that, which individual economising men do, in connection with which there are the well understood individual's own interests and the competition regulating the forces. It is the task of enterprises to produce goods (products or services) for which there is a demand in the market and to sell them at prices, which allow a return on the capital invested for the payment of interest, over and above the covering of the costs, and in doing so permit the long term security of the undertaking.

Entrepreneurial dealing strives as a rule for a multiplicity of aims with, for example, reference to, at a given time or a given period, the largest possible market share, the highest possible productivity, the highest possible profit or cost effectiveness, as the case may be, or for other less well quantifiable aims such as, for instance, the greatest independence or long term security. Additionally, there are social and ecological aims, which are likewise striven for, even though in a measure varying from undertaking to undertaking. Conflicts of targeting spring up in every place where several targets are supposed to be achieved over the same period with the same resources available to hand. In such a situation, the old philosophical question is posed for those carrying the responsibility about the "mean" and the "right measure", with which the different purposes *flow* into the concrete dealing of the undertaking.

---

1 R. GRÖSCHNER: "Zur rechtsphilosophischen Fundierung einer Unternehmensethik", in: H. STEINMANN and A. LÖHR (Eds.): *Unternehmensethik*, Stuttgart (C.E. Poeschel) 1989. pp. 93-113.

To deal responsibly means always and above all to *deal intelligently*, i.e. to weigh up the consequences of one's own actions according to the advantage and the harm that they can provoke. All moral dealings occur on the basis of a weighing up the benefits between the realisation of interests and the avoidance of psychic or social harm, or indeed of damage imposed by the State. From this perspective there is much that figures under the heading "unethical dealing", in the first place unintelligent, indeed on occasion stupid dealing, that is fixed on alleged short term advantages without reflecting on the consequences in the middle and long terms.

The impotence of ethics is proved by the circumstance that most people, faced with economic and political situations requiring a decision, choose to optimise their individual interests and can only be hindered from behaving in a way that is incompatible over a long period with the public weal by a State that proliferates out into many areas of life. A discourse on entrepreneurial ethics has to be always aware of this and precisely on that account aim higher and extend further than merely the avoidance of unintelligent dealings.

II. Perception of Business Ethics

1. Social Perception

If one draws on Holy Scripture for advice, in order to answer the question of whether profit orientated dealing is consistent with actions agreeable to God, then one finds little comfort, for example, in the Book of Jesus Sirach.[2] "It is difficult for a merchant to avoid doing wrong and for a salesman not to incur sin. Many have sinned for the sake of a profit and he who hopes to be rich must be ruthless". Modern commentaries on the compatibility of profit and morals are also rather skeptical on this issue. Thus, the Austrian analyst of contemporary issues, Karl Kraus, is supposed to have replied to the question of a student as to how one could study "economic ethics" that one could not, and that one would have to decide between the two for oneself.

2 Holy Bible, Jerusalem Bible; Ecclesiasticus, or the Wisdom of Jesus the Son of Sirach, Chapter 26 Vers. 29 and Chapter 27 Vers. 1.

With reference to the social perception of business ethics too, it is rather bad: in the past 10-15 years the image that society creates of the private economy and especially of the large corporations is tinged with skeptical uneasiness. Large parts of our society seem to have the impression that a business enterprise cannot have high principles and high profits at the same time. The opinion that many corporations display a deficiency in ethical responsibility and that most firms pursue their profits without scruple as to the cost to the environment, to safety and to the health of consumers is spreading visibly.[3]

This has consequences also for the image of managing personnel: in a survey of the view taken by society of the top professions carried out by the Institute for Demoscopy in Allensbach (Autumn 1993), the top management was classed at rather low ratings:

1.	Doctor	81%
2.	Pastor	40%
3.	Lawyer	36%
4.	University Professor	33%
5.	Diplomat	32%
6.	Author	28%
7.	Pharmacist	27%
8.	Entrepreneur	26%
9.	Engineer	26%
10.	Nuclear Physicist	25%
11.	Primary School Teacher	24%
12.	Director of a Large Firm	22%
13.	Journalist	17%
14.	Graduate Secondary School Teacher	15%

3 Cf. *Business Week* of 29 May 1989, p. 29. From this, according to the results of a representative survey, which the Düsseldorf Institute for Applied Marketing Science carried out in the Federal Republic in 1989, the large giant chemical enterprises seem to be particularly affected: amongst other things, it was asked which enterprise was particularly irresponsible, immoral or unethical. Here 18.8% of those questioned named BASF, 18.2% Bayer, and 12.6% Hoechst. All the same, there were also positive mentions: 5.2% of those questioned cited BASF as particularly exemplary. Here Bayer came in at 2.4% and Hoechst reached 1.9% of the positive mentions. See *Wirtschaftswoche*, No. 5 of 26.1.1990, p. 35.

15.	Officer	9%
16.	Politician	9%
17.	Bookseller	9%
18.	Trade Union Leader	8%

More recent and highly successful publications in the Federal Republic call German managers "flops in pinstripes" and reproach them for "increasing criminalisation"[4] and lawyers talk of a "particularly dangerous potential for power" and of the "criminality of the economically powerful" in connection with the managers of the economy.[5]

2. Self-perception of the Management

Since 1961, surveys to determine the self-perception of the morality of an undertaking have been done over and over again.[6] One result, as a rule, is that nearly all of those management personalities questioned represented the conviction that ethical dealings are profitable in the long term[7], that many however complain that they had to compromise their own values again and again in order to achieve the concern's short term aims.[8] This is particularly the case, according to the perception of lower and middle management, in economically bad times.[9]

4 G. OGGER: *Nieten in Nadelstreifen. Deutschlands Manager in Zwielicht*, München (Droemer Knauer) 1992, p. 67.

5 Quoted in G. EIDAM: *Unternehmen und Strafe. Vorsorge- und Krisenmanagement*, Köln (Carl Heymanns) 1993, p. VII.

6 R. BAUMHART: "How ethical are businessmen?", *Harvard Business Review*, Vol. 39, 4 (1961), pp. 6-19.

7 See also P. ULRICH and U. THIELEMANN: "How do Managers Think about Market Economics and Morality? Empirical Enquiries into Business-ethical Thinking Patterns", *Journal of Business Ethics*, Vol. 12, 11 (1993), pp. 879-898.

8 See also, for example, S.J. VITELL and D.L. DAVIS: "The Relationship between Ethics and Job Satisfaction: An Empirical Investigation", *Journal of Business Ethics*, 9 (1990), pp. 489-494.

9 See also H. BECKER and D.J. FRITSCHE: "Business Ethics: A Cross-cultural Comparison of Managers' Attitudes", *Journal of Business Ethics*, Vol. 6, 4 (1987), pp 289-295, likewise J.A. WATERS Catch 20.5: "Corporate Morality

Statements from members of the topmost levels of management point, in this respect, to a more sympathetic appreciation of the ethical standing of their enterprise —for most of them "all's well with the world".[10] Since the identification between one's own personality and the 'Firm' increases mainly with the steps taken up the ladder of the hierarchy, this is not surprising. Evidence for an ethically higher quality among top management, in comparison with, for example, middle management, should not, however, be adduced from this: potential clarification is to be sought in two directions, for one, in the shifting of moral annoyances 'downwards', for another in possible deficiencies of perception which might occur, or losses of actuality of perception, as the case may be.[11]

It is also interesting that the causes for this erosion of ethical standards in enterprises mostly refer to 'out there' (for example, to lower standards in society, corrupt politicians, etc.); Possibilities for improvement, however, are sought for preference in the enterprises themselves (for example, top management is supposed to give business ethics a higher priority, improving management training, etc.).[12]

---

as an Organizational Phenomenon", *Organizational Dynamics* (American Management Association), Spring 1978, p. 4f; likewise J. MERAN: "Wir haben wirklich andere Sorgen. Unternehmensethik im Zeichen der Rezession", in: Forum für Philosophie (Ed.): *Markt und Moral. Die Diskussion um die Unternehmensethik*, Bern/Stuttgart/Wien (Paul Haupt) 1994, pp. 269-290.

10 B.Z. POSNER and W.H. SCHMIDT: "Ethics in American Companies: A Managerial Perspective", *Journal of Business Ethics*, Vol. 6, 5 (1987), p. 384.

11 Cf. D. HOCHSTÄTTER: "Lorbeer und Mammon", *Wirtschaftwoche*, 5 (26.1.1990), p. 38.

12 See, for example, S.J. VITELL and T.A. FESTERVAND: "Business Ethics: Conflicts, Practices and Beliefs of Industrial Executives", *Journal of Business Ethics*, 6 (1987), pp. 111-122; likewise, M.A. KONOVSKY and F. JASTER: "'Blaming the Victim' and other Ways Business Men and Women Account for Questionable Behaviour", *Journal of Business Ethics*, Vol. 8, 5 (1989), pp. 391-398.

KLAUS M. LEISINGER

III. Business Ethics as a Leadership Task

It is probably indisputable that there does not have to be an 'either-or' link between ethical behaviour and the profitable management of a business. The former Federal Chancellor, *Helmut Schmidt,* was addressing the circumstance, from the point of view of a politician, which is very significant also for those responsible for enterprises: "We must all ask ourselves, how do I get away from what is to what ought to be? In the face of this question, anyone who suggests the shortest straight line as the way, can lead the way to a practical catastrophe. Or the other way round: anyone who follows the shortest path for practical reasons, can unleash an ethical catastrophe".

In what way can a concern successfully overcome the daily ethical challenges? In my opinion, at three levels with various instruments: firstly, with healthy commonsense, or 'moral sense', secondly by means of guidelines for the enterprise and, thirdly, with an integrated staff policy as well as with appropriate Management Development.

1. Moral Common Sense

One can derive a moral sense from basic norms, which were of significance for all cultures from ancient times, for example:

the Golden Rule in its active or passive form,
Kant's Categorical Imperative or
the Categorical Imperative of Hans Jonas.

The following rules of thumb, which Goodpaster recommends under the title "The Moral Common Sense"[13] are of significance here:

Avoid harming others.
Respect the rights of others.
Do not lie or cheat.

---

13 K.E. GOODPASTER: *Ethics in Management*, Boston (Harvard Business School) 1984, p. 6.

Keep promises and contracts.
Obey the law.
Prevent harm to others.
Help those in need.
Be fair.
Reinforce these imperatives in others.

At first glance these 'Nine Commandments' carry so much conviction that a deeper discussion seems unnecessary. Since, however, the keeping alone of these rules of thumb does not always fulfil the moral imperatives under all conditions and as the Goodpaster norms have very varying degrees of obligation, a couple of aspects of the "morally healthy" commonsense ought to be looked at more closely.

Avoid harming others

This is without doubt a norm of obligation, at least as far as its intention goes. In practice it cannot always be observed in this absolute form in many cases. If one takes, for example, as a background to the discussion, the work of the pharmaceutical industry, then the highest recognition is owed to the Hippocratic priority —above all to cause no harm. Medicaments are no normal 'merchandise', for which a "the consumer sovereignty" applies, such as exists otherwise for normal consumer goods. People who, (must) take medicines are either sick and want to get well or must battle, for instance, with incurable diseases against symptoms or pain. The decisions of responsible persons in pharmaceutical concerns (and of similar people in the Registration Authorities) have, under these circumstances, effects not just for the enterprise concerned and its staff, but also for the sick people who have nothing to do with the enterprise. For this reason, stemming from its intention, the avoidance of harm is an obligatory norm for people suffering from an illness.

From this a result for the internationally operating pharmaceutical corporation is that it is a non-negotiable manner of dealing, that between industrialised countries and the states in the course of development, qualitatively essential differences are unacceptable, for instance standards which have to do with safety considerations in production or with the products themselves, with the information on medicaments (indications, side effects, warning notices) and other matters, which are of importance for health or even for the preservation of human life.

As, however, the wholly overwhelmingly greater number of medicaments known today have not only effects but also side effects and these in their turn can impair in varying degree the very health of patients, the injunction "Avoid harming others" refers only to harm avoidable by means of careful actions. Where these cannot be avoided, there exists an obligation for the doctor and the manufacturer of the medicament to provide information, so that at least something approaching consumer sovereignty arises: the acceptance of 'harm' by fully informed patients, who voluntarily give their consent to acceptance of the risks involved, depends very much on the benefits which are hoped for from taking such medicaments. It is self-evident that one is prepared to take the most serious and long-lasting side effects into account, when taking medicine to ward off a fatal disease, whereas one would hardly be ready to tolerate even just the scantiest and temporary side effects when taking something against a cold or with merely cosmetic preparations.

Where 'side-effects' of the most varied kind are not avoidable with even the most careful handling, the exact text of the commandment has to be widened to, for example, "In the achieving of an ethically legitimate goal, prescribe the necessary treatments and medicines so as to cause for others the least possible harm, where it is no longer avoidable by extra care and it is done to the best of one's own knowledge and belief".

Respect the rights of others

People everywhere in the world have the same intrinsic value. Therefore their interests, desires and claims have to be protected to a like degree. In the face of the debated consequences to the environment of the life style of the rich minority on earth, a life style which is not universally realisable, the injunction "Respect the rights of others" is also a 'Norm of Obligation'. In practice, however, to observe it over a long period can be linked to a series of difficulties, for instance in the case of clinical trials of a pharmaceutical enterprise in a developing country.

Theoretically, the scientific demands which are made on clinical trials ought to be equally high in developing countries as they are in industrial countries. The practical prevailing conditions, however, are more often than not completely different in respect of quality. Thus, there are often substantial differences to be seen in the quality of the training of clinical and scientific personnel as well as in the technical infrastructure. These are deficiencies which can significantly diminish the meaningfulness of clinical trials and thus of the certainty of the outcome for future patients.

Further problems can be posed in connection with the willingness of those taking part in the trials. They are very poor, so the financial lure for taking part in a clinical trial can present so great a temptation that it can no longer be a matter of "voluntariness" in the real sense of the word.

Nevertheless, in many cases clinical trials are absolutely necessary for the safety of patients in developing countries, since different genetic, dietetic and other data have important effects on metabolism and thereby on the safety of medicaments. Keeping the commandment "Respect the rights of others", therefore, can lead under the conditions prevailing in economically and socially underdeveloped countries to a more excessive range of unreasonable demands being made than is normally the case in industrialised countries. In the case of clinical trials to be carried out in an exemplary manner, this could, for instance, be by an internationally staffed watchdog committee, which guarantees credible prevailing conditions and results.

Do not lie or cheat

In connection with this, the 'three dog-theory' is of interest: a man rings at the door of a house and says to the person who opens it "*Your dog has bitten me*". The reaction according to the 'first dog-theory' is "*We have no dog*". That, of course, is the very moment when the incriminating hound comes running and barking round the house. Now the 'second dog-theory' comes into operation, namely with the words "*It's true that we have a dog, but this one doesn't bite*". The last word had hardly been spoken, when the dog bit the poor man at the door yet again. Well all that remains is only the 'third dog-theory': "*We do have a dog. Now and again he even bites —but it doesn't hurt*".

According to this theory, the disadvantage of the process is that the credibility of the action gets lower and lower at each stage. The uninvolved observer must gain the impression that only what has, in any case, been proven will be admitted. In this manner a 'conjecture gap' arises: even when everything has been said and granted, one is left waiting for the 'fourth dog'. Where trust in the correctness of the information has disappeared, even the truth in the end has problems of credibility —or, as is said in the vernacular, "Whoever tells a lie once is not believed, even if he is speaking the truth".

A piece of bad luck, that entered the law-books as 'the Rose Monday case' may make the practical relevance of the 'three dog-theory' understandable. Following an accident at the works, the firm concerned announced that the 'yellow rain, which fell on populated city districts on the morning of 22 February 1992 had minor toxicity'. After complaints by the residents the amount was corrected upwards and, following investigations by Greenpeace it had to be admitted in the end that it was several tonnes of a mixture of 11 different substances, of which the o-nitroanisol, similarly emitted could be regarded as a cause of cancer.[14] Analogous situations have also been observed in connection with the information about unexpected side effects of medicaments and about other items of bad news, received with defensive reactions by implied targets.

"Do not lie or cheat" means in the practice of business "Tell the whole truth and nothing other than this". This means the fullest avoidance of all known 'informational pathologies'[15] (within and without the concern) and, where this is the case, even the avoidance of an admission that something is not or not yet known. Of course, in such cases, up-to-date current information about the changed state of knowledge and concentrated efforts are required, to place at disposal all available resources for making good deficiencies in knowledge.

Semantic clarity is a final requirement in this connection: Katherine Riley points out that there is a range of possibilities of speaking the truth in a way that leads to error and, by other means, to dodge clear communication, that is not subject to misunderstanding.[16] By this means, defective interpretations and lack of understanding are fostered. It is therefore useful for the benefit of the ethical side to replace the injunction 'Do not lie or cheat' by 'Tell the truth and nothing but the truth and this in a way that is clear and not capable of being misunderstood'.

Such an information policy also corresponds to common sense, for a policy of naively claiming not to understand, of not wanting to admit a

---

14 On this, see G. EIDAM: *Unternehmen und Strafe. Vorsorge- und Krisenmanagement*, Köln (Carl Heymanns) 1993, pp. 191, 403, 421.

15 On this, see St. SORG: "Informationspathologien und Erkenntnisfortschritt in Organisationen". München (Planning and Organisation Sciences Writings of Munich University) 1982.

16 K. RILEY: "Telling more than the truth: Implicature, Speech Acts and Ethics in Professional Communication", *Journal of Business Ethics*, Vol. 12, 3 (1993), pp. 179-196.

thing, of tranquillising the public, of playing the innocent and of tardy disclosure of facts, the catalogue of deficiencies as well as of omissions only under pressure from the public, as was practised in many cases in the past, cannot be maintained by any institution over a long period and it can cause immense damage to its credibility.

Be fair

As already mentioned, individual and collective human dealings have also to be so fashioned in the context of an undertaking that we can commit ourselves to it [prescriptivity] but also be ready at the same time to accept it as a model for a principle for actions, which also has to be valid as a prescription for others in similar circumstances [universalisability].[17]

As evident as this statement is, so can "real existing" people end up in situations in their everyday workplaces, for instance, in which they act unjustly or, at the very least, unfairly. For a better understanding of this statement, two examples ought to serve:

Imagine that there is a young woman working in your department with out of the ordinary intelligence and the capability to put this to action in a disciplined way with results in the works. Let us assume that this person contributes quite disproportionately to the success of your department and you benefit from this not only with your bonus but soon probably by promotion in the hierarchy. Now you hear one day that another department is showing great interest in this woman. Because of a reorganisation the opportunity is offered for this woman to occupy a new important position. She would benefit from it significantly, both financially and in her career. The final decision, however, so you hear, depends absolutely on your personal appraisal of this woman and your recommendation.

Do you deal with this situation as you should do in order to act justly (and also as would lie in the superordinate interests of the firm), in the face of the fact that you, by doing so, cause potential harm to your department and to yourself? Of course, you do the right thing, for you are, to be sure, a just man and act according to the 'Golden Rule'

How is it though in the following case? Let us assume that you had over many years a colleague, who makes himself unappreciated not only by reason

---

17 R.M. HARE: "Eine moderne Form der 'Goldenen Regel'", in: D. BIRNBACHER and N. HOERSTER (Eds.): *Texte zur Ethik*, München (dtv) 1987, p. 110ff.

of his being below average intelligence and with a defective attitude to work but, over and above that, from the fact that he is an encumbrance to the climate of the department by reason of his arrogant and know-all manner as well as for his gossiping about his colleagues. Let us assume further that all your attempts to shift this fellow-worker into other positions fail, because an officially recognised impediment also involves dismissal with many attendant difficulties. Everything points to the fact that you are going to have to live with him to the end of your days.

Now you hear by chance that a competitor's corporation is showing an interest in this person. On this occasion too, however, your assessment will be sought before a concrete offer is made to the person. How will you act? To be just you would have to tell the truth when questioned and thus seal your own fate. A sympathetically tinted even, to some extent, an enthusiastic assessment would, however, free you from a staff problem that has gone on for years...

To exercise justice —not only against your own interest but also in respect of others can be coupled with unpleasant consequences in private practice and in the practices of firms.

A final commandment of Goodpaster's that should be illustrated here is:

Reinforce these imperatives in others

In connection with this, for example, the question of replying is on the agenda as to under what circumstances it is morally commanded that an enterprise summon up the courage to take over the responsibility to manage instead of —as is often the case— joining the time wasting search for 'coalition-solutions' that are based on a broad consensus. 'Coalition-solutions', from experience, often present the lowest common denominator and most remain well behind what would be possible for an individual enterprise, which requires qualitative 'leadership' in specific circumstances. Not that there would be no arguments for a concerted 'branch' procedure, where the common weal is better served by improved joint dealings than through heroic individual acts. Where, however, within enterprises, immediate responsibility for staff postings is recommended, where there are ethically relevant questions, 'coalition-solutions' are only the second-best choice.

Anyone who, because of better knowledge or more highly developed consciousness of responsibility recognises the danger, the avoidance of which is possible and reasonable, has also the moral duty to make others aware of it and, by doing so, speed up a change in the *status quo*. Positive social change of every kind started with a change of actions by a small minority.

In addition to healthy moral common sense, there is a second element for the shifting of ethical considerations into the activities of a business, namely guidelines for sensitive matters in the undertaking.

2. Codes of Conduct for Sensitive Matters

As has already been said, not everything that is legal is also legitimate. An enterprise that is operating internationally, which has to come to grips with various legal and social structural conditions, specific to the different countries, but is striving for concordant ethical standards, is well advised to work out guidelines for the enterprise, which cover all the sensitive areas of its activities. There is no *a priori* harmony between the economic advantage to the enterprise, or to the individual as the case may be, and what is to be preferred from the point of view of society. Rather there is a range of potential conflicts, which it is worthwhile to minimise with the enterprise's ethical deliberations.

Guidelines of an undertaking are defined here as behavioural norms, which are put into practice by the undertaking not under the compulsion of the law but which are, nevertheless, binding on all fellow-workers, in order to minimise potential conflicts, which arise as a consequence of undesired effects of normal business activity for society and the environment. Such guidelines by an undertaking make it clear that it is not a matter of indifference to the management as to how the business targets are achieved. At the very least, what is considered to be clearly unacceptable behaviour in the undertaking is held in the undertaking's guidelines to be out of the question in the sense of its being an example of negative ethics. Here too, the words of Wilhelm Busch are apposite. "All the good beneath the sun is always bad you haven't done".

To the sensitive specialist areas belong, for example, marketing, information policy, environmental protection, business activities in and with developing countries, trials involving animals, research policy or, according to the branch, other matters. In this, an ethically acceptable range for action should be mapped out, as well as an analysis of the effects on men, the environment and society. In a phase of evaluation and weighing up, then the desirable and what is undesirable have to be determined and formulated.

As not just undertakings but probably all institutions on this earth have had, for a long time, the tendency to be self-referrential, i.e. to live in a rather closed system of values and interests, it is important that the guidelines for undertakings rest on a far-reaching social consensus. Therefore they ought to reflect not only the philosophy of the undertaking, lived by the top management but also have passed the acid test of independent criticism from outside the business, before they are agreed, and, as far as is ever possible, be a result of consensual dialogue.

The decision processes are difficult, which incorporate informed opinion from persons outside the enterprise, who wish to bring their concerns and interests into solutions but make their judgements according to criteria which are other than economic ones and whose ethical judgement takes account of other grounds for evaluation.[18] For one thing, dialogues are "open processes", i.e. the outcome cannot be planned in advance and the effects and consequences are manageable to only a limited extent. For another dialogues do not automatically lead to agreement and the danger arises that they get out of hand by becoming endless and become drawn into ever less relevant controversies, instead of agreeing on a compromise acceptable to both sides for the practical work.

Nevertheless, controversies must be settled. Although the ultimate authority for decisions about matters of the undertaking's policy rests in the undertaking itself and cannot be shifted outside it, a harmonisation of controversial points of view during discourse is more capable of prospective realisation than one imposed by force. All those taking part must be in a position to renounce claims to superiority, to rethink their own position and —if necessary— to abandon it. Candour and pluralism are a requirement but not 'à-la-carte' choices or cheap tolerance for the avoidance of disputes.

Guiding lines on sensitive matters by enterprises are, naturally, not a standardised 'Manual for ethical dealings', after the reading of which borderline situations in all sorts of cases can be overcome in an ethically acceptable way. Rich, in particular, points to the fact that the basic ethical

18 In spite of all the differences as to value-attitudes, a minimum consensus regarding the common accepted values is, nevertheless, required, otherwise a dialogue can have no constructive consequences. Fundamentalist positions of 'never''and 'under no circumstances' cannot be bound into compromises.

questions are "wherever they become concrete, always questions, to which there is no single, smooth answer, which will harmonize the conflict and calm the trouble".[19] Nevertheless, guidelines of the kind mentioned here can give the employees of a company a basis for the setting of priorities when commercial decisions have to be made under pressure of time and financial constraints.

Moreover, guiding lines of this kind and their continuously checked compliance still offer no danger to the implementation of the enterprise's ethical ambitions. Johann Heinrich Pestalozzi pointed out nearly 200 years ago that no form of government in a country can be much good, if its people are a real bad lot. Werner Lachmann carried this thinking over into a context of commercial structures, that function as well "as the people, who do dealings within it".[20] It only remains here to add: the best corporate policies and codes of conduct are only as good as the management which applies them. They have credibility and thus power to conduct matters only when an enterprise does more than merely distribute them internally as a pamphlet or manual.[21] On this account the selection of suitable staff is of greater importance for the implementation of the enterprise's ethical ambitions.

3. Personnel Policy and Management Development

Max Weber, the eminent German sociologist, at the very beginning of this century, alluded in the following words to the particular responsibility of managers: "People who must make political or economic decisions on matters that affect other people's lives will, unless they have lost all reason, find themselves forced more and more to evaluate not only their ethical motivations, but also their decisions' likely consequences based on their knowledge and conscience."

My naiveté does not go as far as to believe that we average mortals could do justice in everyday life to the ideal that the Sermon on the Mount or important texts of other religions pass on to us. When we are convinced,

---

19 A. RICH: *Wirtschaftsethik, Grundlagen in theologischer Perspective*, Vols. 1, 3., Gütersloh (Gerd Mohn) 3rd ed. 1987, p. 18.

20 W. LACHMANN: *Wirtschaft und Ethik*, Stuttgart (Hänseler) 1987, p.10.

21 H.L. PITT and K.A. GROSKAUFMANIS: "Why a Corporate Code may not protect you", in: Conference Board (Ed.): *Across the Board*, May 1990, pp. 22-25.

though, that profits, turnover or other entrepreneurial success can never be an end in themselves, but are legitimate only when they are in the service of people and the community, then the criteria also for personnel selection and the content of Management Development ought to be widened to take in the ideal.

a) The Significance of Primary Virtues

Already with the analysis of the classical texts on ethics, we draw near to the ideal structure of personality and the desirable attributes of character among those bearing responsibility, for since men began to think the (nostalgic) 'requirement profile' is somewhat comparable with that for 'emperors', 'kings', 'field commanders', 'governors' —or, likewise, for managers too. Here a look back is worthwhile, whether to the recommended way of Laotse[22], to the conversations of Kungfutse (Confucius)[23], the Indian secret Upanishads teachings[24] or to Plato[25], who (in his *Politeia*) describes Reason, developed into Wisdom, Justice, Courage and Thoughtfulness as the most important virtues, but also to Max Weber and his statements on "Politics as a Profession".[26]

Under the *primary virtues* today are understood —in addition to the traditional *cardinal virtues*— such virtues as Justice, Courage, Moderation and Prudence, which one can paraphrase with the concepts of Moral Courage, Competence in Conflict, Tolerance and readiness to undertake Constructive Disobedience.[27] Of particular importance in this connection —and not, by a long way, just for enterprises but for institutions of every kind— is practised Moral Courage.

---

22 LAOTSE: *Tao te King*, Zürich (Diogenes) 1985.

23 KUNGFUTSE: *Gespräche - Lun Yü*, Köln (Eugen Diedrichs Verlag, Diedrichs Gelbe Reihe) 1987.

24 UPANISHADEN: *Die Geheimlehre der Inder*, Köln (Eugen Diedrichs Verlag, Diedrichs Gelbe Reihe) 1986.

25 PLATO: *Der Staat. (Politeia)*, München (Deutscher Taschenbuch Verlag/ Artemis, Bibliothek der Antike) 1991.

26 M. WEBER: "Politik als Beruf", in: M. WEBER: *Gesammelte Politische Schriften* , Tübingen (J.C.B. MOHR UTB [Paul Siebeck]) 5th ed. 1988, pp. 505-560.

27 Cf. R. LAY: *Die Macht der Moral: Unternehmenserfolg durch ethisches Management*, Düsseldorf (Econ Taschenbuch) 1993, p. 22.

It is not that everyone would be born to be a resistance hero in totalitarian systems and would have to put his or her existence into play for a just cause —measured resistance starts at a lower level. Joachim Gauck, the Federal Commissioner for the State Security files of the former GDR, indicated in a comparable association at a symposium arranged by the ZEIT-magazine on the occasion of the 75th birthday of Helmut Schmidt, that the first step towards resistance is to learn to refuse to be enthusiastic. Once again this holds true not just for totalitarian states but also for institutions of every type.

For practised moral courage in enterprises, jurisprudence has already 25 years ago, set down markers for the individual acts of people carrying responsibilities. In the final decision of the *Contergan* [Engl. *Thalidomide*] trial, the Provincial Court in Aachen in December 1970 established the following, with reference to *personal guilt* owing to the lack of moral courage in the accused fellow-workers of the firm affected, "Neither do personal difficulties lead on to the fact that more extensive actions would not have been, to a degree, reasonable. In the face of the significance of the threatening danger of serious health damage, relatively small, to be sure, in comparison with the use of the drug, to a number measured against the absolute number but a still not insignificant circle of people, it was to be demanded of them that they took personal difficulties into account in an emergency situation. In this the requirement was not excessive. Otherwise, the health of many people would have been open to being put at risk."[28]

The analysis of all great catastrophes of recent years shows that, long before the Challenger incident, the Chernobyl catastrophe or the Exxon-Valdez disaster, there were critical voices and warning indications regarding the weak points that would come to the surface later. However, no notice was taken of them or they were smoothed over. More moral courage at all levels carries the greatest weight among the desirable attributes of those who bear responsibility, as a defence of the relevant criticism, binding in the form, but hard in the actual case.

With a discriminating selection of personnel, there can be much influence granted to the fact that those who work for an enterprise and represent it, both within it and outside of it, have certain essential aspects in their personality. In the best case, by means of this, personalities are to be found, with those

28 See J. SCHMIDT-SALZER: *Entscheidungssammlung; Produkthaftung*. Vol. II, Berlin 1979, p. 48ff and Vol. IV, München 1982, p. 271ff.

qualities of character that we would wish for ourselves among people, on whose decisions depend our own prosperity and that of our families. These would be managements, which are aware of their full responsibility for all that they do or refrain from doing —people with such virtues as modesty, sensitivity, consciousness of social responsibility and the capability of taking an overall view of things. Max Weber's differentiation between 'the ethic of attitude' and the 'ethics of responsibility' are consistently relevant in this connection.[29]

29 See, on this point M. WEBER: *Politik als Beruf. Op. cit.* p. 551 ff. For Max Weber the ethics of the Sermon on the Mount (for instance, 'offer him the other cheek') were not binding, except for saints. For politicians, what would have to be much more binding would be "thou shalt oppose Evil with violence, otherwise thou art responsible for its increase" (p. 551). And, further, "we must be clear that all ethically orientated actions can stand under two maxims, which are basically different from one another and are mutually incapable of settlement; it can be the 'ethics of conviction' or the 'ethics of responsibility'. It is not that the ethics of conviction would be identical with irresponsibility or the ethics of responsibility with unscrupulousness. It is, though, an abysmal conflict as to whether one is responsible under the maxim of the ethics of conviction —expressed in religious terms, "the Christian does what is right and leaves the outcome up to God" or one must answer for the (foreseeable) consequences of one's actions under the maxim of the ethics of responsibility. If the consequences of the flow of one's actions, arising purely from the ethics of conviction, are evil, then for him (the moral philosopher) it is not the author of the actions who is responsible but the world, or other people's stupidity or the will of God, who created it that way. The moral philosopher of the ethics of responsibility school reckons precisely from an adversarial standpoint with those average defects of mankind —he has, as Fichte has rightly said, no right whatsoever to presuppose their goodness and perfection, he does not feel in a position to shuffle off onto others the consequences of his own doings, insofar as he could foresee them. He will say "these consequences are attributable to me". The moral philosopher of the ethics of responsibility school feels 'responsible' only for the flame of pure conviction not being extinguished, the flame, for example, of protest against the injustice of the social order. Constantly to rekindle it anew is the purpose of his deeds".

b) The Significance of Secondary Virtues

Now a few words on the *secondary virtues* after the emphasis given to the *primary* ones. Semantically, there is already a taste of depreciation attached to the words 'secondary virtue'. The contemptuous belittlement of secondary virtues may perhaps serve to deal in a flirtatious way with one or the other but it is not right. What are being addressed, of course, are ideals and attitudes to life, such as obedience, loyalty, efficiency, love of order, honourable dealing, thrift, reliability, cleanliness, punctuality and also those ideals and attitudes to life that belong to the basic presuppositions for the success of the early industrial development of Europe and North America, and that today are among the pillars, supporting the economic success of the Asian 'tiger economies'.

The ' vanishing of a sense of duty' is a problematic concomitant of modern life, for problems are not to be solved by 'self-realisation', 'gratification' and 'new meditation'; they are simply talked out of existence. It is precisely in connection with discussions about proficiency in the light of international competition and the safeguarding of industrial positions that it is not possible —notwithstanding all the validity of primary virtues— to point out sufficiently clearly the great importance of the 'secondary virtues'. It remains beyond dispute, of course, that secondary virtues can only be richly blessed in association with the primary ones.

Enduring entrepreneurial success with, for instance, the Asian tiger economies, whose peoples stand out by reason of their diligence, discipline, good training and modest demands is not achievable without attention to the secondary virtues. Social circumstances, in which people still think about nothing but what they are entitled to but become forgetful about what needs to be done to obtain it (a deficiency in respect of the primary virtue of fairness), these circumstances are an obstacle not only for lasting entrepreneurial success but also for the success of a society. Where the importance of secondary virtues is talked down, the capacity of industrial areas to compete sinks, as does employment as a result of it, at least for those who are not shielded by having permanent established status at work.

c) Management Development

There is controversy as to whether such primary virtues can be taught or learned, as the case may be. Since Immanual Kant, great moral philosophers have pronounced themselves, time and again, to be rather skeptical in the question as to whether mankind was capable of being improved. Kant expressed the opinion, "nothing quite straight can be fashioned out of such warped wood as man is made of."[30] In spite of that, there are no grounds for capitulation. There is a range of positive experiences inclusive of ethical matters in the training plans.[31] Normative orientations in connection with an undertaking's decisions can be taught and learned —even if not so easily as the orthodox content of training and further training courses within an enterprise or superordinate to it. In spite of the difficulties associated with this kind of training, the reflection on questions of value and feelings is extraordinarily significant for the long-term prosperity of the enterprise, as important knowledge about orientations can be passed on —knowledge about orientations in respect of the potentialities and limitations of human dealings and abilities, and this not in the sense of isolated dogma but as a process of an approach with reasoned arguments.

Without doubt, case studies (for example, the parable of Sadhu[32]) as well as the subsequent discussion of the involved circle of ethical problems[33] are valuable. Case studies gain in quality, when ethical dilemmas and the facts of the prisoners' dilemmas are dealt with and they take account of their complex courses, in which comprehensive decisions are divided up into single-item

---

30 See I. KANT: "Ideen zu einer allgemeinen Geschichte in weltbürgerliche Absicht", in: W. WEISCHEDEL (Ed.) *Schriften zur Anthropologie, Geschichtsphilosophie, Politik und Pädagogik*, Werkausgabe Vol. XI. Frankfurt a. M. (Suhrkamp Taschenbuch Wissenschaft) 1968, p. 41. In the same article, however, there is a pointer, from which it would be possible to infer the desire for further moral education: "We are cultivated through art and science to a high degree. We are civilised to the point of overloading in every kind of social civility and decorum; but to consider ourselves to have become schooled in morality, there is still much that is lacking", p. 44 (*ibid*)

31 Cf. for example D.R. NELSON and T.E. OBREMSKI: "Promoting Moral Growth through Intra-Group Participation", *Journal of Business Ethics*, 9 (1990), pp. 731-739; likewise H. JOHNSON: "Bribery in International Markets: Diagnosis, Clarification and Remedy", *Journal of Business Ethics*, 4 (1985), pp. 447-455.

32 See on this: B.H. MCCOY: "The Parable of the Sadhu", *Harvard Business Review*, Sept./Oct. (1983), p. 103ff.

33 See on this: T.H. TYSON: "Believing that Everyone Else is Less Ethical: Implications for Work Behaviour and Ethics Instruction", *Journal of Business Ethics*, 9 (1990), pp. 715-721.

decisions. In such cases it can be demonstrated that while the ethical quality of the many single steps that occur in the course of the action can be harmless at the time, adding together all the many single steps can be so problematical that the inference of the need to reflect each single step from the viewpoint of the whole is inevitable.

'Situational ethics' are of great importance in connection with the discussion of case studies. There are no basic moral principles which are valid under all circumstances. Even the commandment "Thou shalt not kill" is not valid absolutely, if one has to act in self-defence or to prevent greater harm being done. What is ethically good in a specific situation is not to be derived in general from books and guidelines but only where there is intention. Moral decisions are always decisions made in a state of uncertainty and their quality depends on the specific circumstances and on the information and help towards coming to a decision available at that moment. As in by far the greater number of cases no decision for the 'Good' as against the 'Bad' is on the agenda, but the lesser evil has to be sought after in a careful quality appraisal, coming to grips with situational ethics has to be a long lasting affair.

d) Performance Appraisal

The implementation of an enterprise's maxims into its everyday practice is not a 'boss's matter'; it has to be practised at all levels. It is highly probable, however, that it will remain bogged down in good intentions, if appropriate criteria for decision processes are not internalised by the top level of the enterprise's hierarchy and set as credible examples as well as taken account of in the performance appraisals.

In most cases, this means that the catalogue of criteria for performance appraisals and the system of incentives has to be expanded. Moral norms too are all the more effective, the more consistently compliance with them is checked, their observance rewarded or, where applicable, infringements punished. For as long as fellow-workers are measured exclusively by short-term financial results, they could see themselves forced to come to decisions in ethically ambivalent situations in favour of their own financial or (perceived) career advantage and against the voice of their conscience.

Assessments in the sphere of product safety, environmental production, information policy, fairness in personnel policy and other matters not measurable in money units would have a tendency to acquire greater weight in performance appraisals of the management. Ethical patterns of behaviour should, wherever possible, lead to advancement even if the short term gains turn out to be negative. It is also the same the other way round. The significance of ethical norms has also to become visible within an organisation by making clear the fact that men and woman can be demoted immediately or, in serious cases, dismissed even if short-term economic benefit to the firm had come about because of their shortcomings.

To find criteria by which ethical behaviour can be measured is, admittedly, not always easy. Is the fact that a sales manager has not reached his (or her) target or has overstepped the costs budget to be put down to ethical reservations or is such a reproach only an alibi to explain a lack of commitment? Is it a fact that inefficient or idle colleagues can exploit the system and the hard worker fall by the wayside? It is not easy to close up these gaps; it ought to be possible however.

IV. Good Ethics are Good Business

Why should a company consider ethics in directing its behaviour —on top of law, self-interest, and convention? The worst conceivable result of high moral standards would be competitive or other tangible detriment because the special efforts and costs a company attaches to ethical consideration result in net disadvantages for it. There are a number of indications that the short-term profit from ethical conduct does not exactly burst into the limelight or even show clearly measurable financial disadvantages. It would be dishonest to exclude these effects of an enterprise's ethical dealing option.

On the other hand, there are many empirical examples in which unethical corporate behaviour caused a great social outcry and intervention from the authorities, and presented no favourable options even in the short-term.[34] In these cases it is easy to explain that unethical behaviour can be a burden for an enterprise and that high ethical standards can turn out to be worth a fortune.

---

34 See also on this J.R. SWANDA Jr: "Goodwill, Going Concern, Stocks and Flows: A Prescription for Moral Analysis", *Journal of Business Ethics*, 9 (1990), pp. 751-759.

At least for enlightened corporations, commercial success now means more than just how big the year's profit is. Profits to companies are like food to people: an absolute necessity, without which they die. But only a few —sick— people would consider eating to be the central or only purpose of life. The reputation of a company is one of its most valuable assets, even if it does not appear directly in the balance sheet (Swanda therefore suggests that "goodwill" should become a balance-sheet item).[35] The verdict of the public depends significantly on the company's perceived contribution to socially valued ends. Meeting customer requirements in the extended sense, i.e. acting in a socially and environmentally responsible way and using energy and non-renewable resources wisely, are important blocks in the mosaic of commercial success.

It is probable that ethical dealing 'pays for itself' —at least in the middle and long term— and that for the reasons that follow:

1. Reduction of the Costs of Friction with Society

First and foremost, ethical conduct brings reductions in the cost of friction with the social environment (for private individuals and institutions). For corporations, social friction costs arise where behaviour which is legal but seen as illegitimate or unethical leads to calls for boycotts from church or other organisations. Whether a critically committed public demonstrates in front of the works gates, charitable organisations set up wailing walls, or the media "put on pressure" through critical reporting —for the corporation concerned, this means loss in social recognition. Whether this leads to a fall in the share price or physically measurable sales losses occur or not is of secondary importance. Criticism "from outside" generally means that management capacity is taken up with defensive activity and is therefore not free for the shaping of the future. Intelligent corporations forbid dealings that could provoke negative social reactions.

On the other hand, there is growing evidence that a corporation's "image" can become a competitive advantage because a "positive coefficient" arises.[36] This can become a decisive market advantage where an enterprise offers

35 *Ibid.*

36 See on this, GLOBAL BUSINESS RELATION (Ed.): "The International Business Issues Monitor", *Monitor Bulletin* # 90-19, New York 1990.

products and services, which are comparable with those of other corporations in quality and utility. In the USA there is a range of indications that so-called 'green consumers' form an increasingly important niche in the markets and firms which behave in an exemplary manner, ecologically speaking, over and above the legal regulations, gain market advantages from this.

2. Employees' Motivation

Other costs can arise through friction with one's own employees. The fact that a company is the focus of public criticism (but also in a situation where employees see that colleagues are promoting their careers in an unethical way) can have disastrous results for morale and job satisfaction in a corporation. In the mid- and long-term, this can lead to valuable employees looking for other work and leaving the corporation. As employees are a corporation's most valuable "capital", this alone is reason enough why unethical conduct cannot lie in a corporation's interests.

The fact that corporate behaviour which is at least frictionless but wherever possible goes beyond marginal ethics also prompts customers to buy and motivates serious investors to purchase shares, and that the direct neighbours (residents, communities) look to the corporation with pleasure and pride reinforces employees' positive identification. What Jakob Burckhardt formulated for individuals also applies to whole corporations: they are not just what they are, but also what they have set themselves as ideals. Even if they do not emulate these one hundred per cent, a part of their being is marked by the mere fact of wanting to.[37]

3. Attractiveness of the Enterprise as an Employer

There is a series of clues in the fact that enterprises, which are perceived as ethically above reproach, are more attractive as employers than those, which are criticised among the public on account of their being lacking in awareness of their responsibilities or even on account of deliberate damage to

---

37 J. BURCKHARDT: *Griechische Kulturgeschichte.* Cited in: A. RIKLIN: *Politische Ethik.* Vorträge der Aeneas-Silvius-Stiftung at Basel University, Basel (Helbing & Lichtenhahn) 1987.

the common weal or to the environment. In a survey, which the Basel Prognos AG Company carried out among men and women students of the economic sciences in 1990, on important criteria for reasons for coming to a decision about a workplace, 88% gave 'enjoyment of the work', 67% a 'good working atmosphere' and 66% 'sensible activity' —all factors, which are hardly to be found, where Greenpeace is protesting in front of the factory gates or churches are calling for a boycott.

Nowadays, enterprises are no longer only measured by what they produce but also by what they demonstrate. The force of such trends, naturally, can change again, above all when the situation of the employment market develops not to the favour of those looking for work, but a growing number of citizens, whether as salaried employees or as customers alike, are taking ethical points of view seriously —even more seriously than was the case 10 or 20 years ago.

4. Protection of Entrepreneurial Freedom

Many of those who carry responsibility in enterprises nowadays complain about an excessively high and even growing density of regulations through laws, orders and stipulations. The freedom of entrepreneurs could —so goes the continuing complaint— be no longer actualised inside an ever more narrowly tightened corset of instructions from the State. Too high a density of regulations endangers the position. There is much that indicates that such complaints have a real basis in all sorts of ways and that 'less State' (or a "leaner" State) could have a stimulating effect on corporate commitment.

Freedom is, however, always freedom as ethical duty and may thus be demanded only as a correlate of responsibility. Anyone who wishes to help avoid further reglementation of the economy and correct inappropriate legal developments must offer plausible proof of ethically responsible conduct.

Ethically responsible corporate dealings mean dealings beyond the *status quo*, active shaping, and forward-looking ethical equilibration. Whoever maintains a running battle on the basis of current law to defend positions that might have been based on a consensus many years ago but which are now regarded as illegitimate and will be even more so in the future, is not being businesslike but negligent. Such companies support those social forces that demand more controls, narrower legislative chains, and thus more state bureaucracy.

5. Applied Business Ethics as a Comprehensive Competitive Advantage

Innovation, efficiency, effectiveness, the capacity to exploit market potential to the full and to interpret the signs of the times as well as the art, at the right time and right place, of saving costs and expenditure, will along with all the other entrepreneurial virtues be of the highest importance in the future too. A further element will grow in significance however, i.e. applied entrepreneurial ethics. They are becoming ever more a new, solid foundation of the capability to compete, which oversteps the bounds of classical markets. The greater the prosperity of a society becomes, the more non-material values gain in significance. Undertakings which deal ethically for all to see, come to be more and more preferred by their customers. This fact is becoming a problem for those enterprises which ignore moral ways of looking at a matter; for others it becomes an opportunity to get to the top.

Part Three

Mass Media and Ethics

Chapter 5

Philosophy in an Age of Overinformation

VITTORIO HÖSLE

I. The Problem of Overinformation

That the information bits we are confronted with do increase every day, is one of the few things all of us can still know —even if an immediate consequence of this insight is that what we can individually know is a less and less part of what is known by contemporary world culture as a whole. The exponential growth of informations takes place at two different levels. On the one hand, more and more new facts are discovered in the single sciences. The mathematical intelligence of Archimedes was inferior to the intelligence of, if any, only very few mathematicians of our time; but if we compare the amount of the mathematical knowledge mastered by the Greek culture with that mastered by ours, the distance is immense. Even the average mathematics professor nowadays knows much more than Archimedes, not to speak of the combination of the knowledge of all living mathematics professors compared with the knowledge of all Greek mathematicians. And since also history of mathematics is an interesting topic, we cannot even say that at least contemporary knowledge replaces the knowledge the past had acquired. The former works of mathematics continue to constitute a subject of study, even if the historical interest with which we approach them has a different nature than the immediate, systematic interest which wants to learn from and not about an author. Therefore with the flow of time the amount of things to know automatically grows, even in the case there is no substantial progress in knowledge.

On the other hand, also the life world has to face an information flood unknown to all past cultures. This has partly to do with the fact that the new insights of the different sciences are passed on to the general public in a diluted form, thanks to new and new media of communication, as book, radio and television. But popular formulations of the sciences at all conceivable levels do not constitute the bulk of the informations which threaten us. Modern democracy and civil society presuppose the ideology (be it true or not) that the majority of the citizens be well-informed about the main decisions the government or other power centers have to take. Therefore we hear or read, or at least can hear or read, several times every day about natural catastrophes nearby and far away, about sexual scandals in which actors, MPs and the few members of royal houses still existing are involved, about the development of exchange rates between the different valutas. The logic of the mass media system which has become itself one of the most influential power centers in the modern world forces it to produce more and more information bits. An example to which many others could be added is particularly enlightening. The time dedicated to the news is every evening the same, although it is not very likely that every day the same amount of important events takes place, and therefore on objectively empty days information bits have to be passed on that on other days would be neglected: The form determines the content.

But the alteration of politics caused by the new information system is not the subject of my lecture, as important as it is. I am interested, first, in the impact the new information system has on philosophy (I). In fact it is obvious that contemporary philosophy differs quite profoundly from what philosophy has been in the past, and it is easy to see that one, if not the central, cause of these differences is the new informational environment within which philosophy nowadays has to live and from which it has to select the material necessary for its own constructions. But diagnosis is not enough. If there is something which remains in the sphere of philosophy, irreducible to the competence of the single sciences, it is the normative realm; and therefore after diagnosis therapeutical proposals are necessary. We cannot limit ourselves to understanding what modern philosophy has become and why it has become what it is; we need also a concept of what philosophy ought to be, and must reflect on how it could regain its essence in an age of overinformation (II). Particularly the following question has to be answered: Which informations should philosophers try to select in our time in order to fulfill their task seriously?

II. Philosophy as Social Subsystem

Whether philosophy can or cannot be called a science, is a question differently answered by various philosophers, partly in dependance on the connotations the word "science" respectively the corresponding word in other languages has. "Science" denoting mainly the natural sciences in the English language, one would tend to a negative answer when one faces the question in English; in German "Wissenschaft" including also the "Geisteswissenschaften", the answer is usually positive. In any case philosophy is a very atypical science, for it does not have as object a limited sphere of being, as the other sciences have. But nobody will deny that is a form of knowledge, an epistemic system, and as such it can be analysed according to two different models. Thus the concept of science and of knowledge implies a normative moment —not everything which calls itself "knowledge" is knowledge; there are certain criteria that have to be fulfilled in order to deserve this title. The justification of these criteria is one of the greatest problems of epistemology. Already ancient skepticism has tried to show the insolubility of this problem, arguing that the criteria that ought to justify the rationality of a proof have themselves to be proved, so that a circle be inevitable.[1] I do not share skepticism's pessimism, even if here is not the place to develop a criticism of the presuppositions implied by the criterion argument.[2] One thing, however, is obvious: If there is no possibility of a non-circular grounding of the last criteria of science and knowledge, the temptation is almost irresistible to accept as legitimate criterion what is regarded as such by the usual practice of the science or epistemic system. Wittgenstein's famous argument against the possibility of a private language is based on the diffidence against the possibility of a rational answer to the question what it means to follow a rule.[3] Such an answer is still an epistemological, albeit a skeptical one.

---

1 One need only read Diogenes Laertius and Sextus on the five tropes of Agrippa, as well as Sextus' second book of the *Pyrrhoneioi hypotyposeis* and the first two books of *Adversus dogmaticos*.

2 Cf. V. HÖSLE: "Foundational Issues of Objective Idealism", *Graduate Faculty Philosophy Journal*, 17 (1994), pp. 245-287.

3 Cf. S.A. KRIPKE: *Wittgenstein on Rules and Private Languages*, Cambridge, Mass. (Harvard University Press)1982.

We shift, however, our intellectual interest if we give up the normative question and try to analyse the social system called science or knowledge in its relation with other social systems, without any normative pretensions whatsover. That is what sociology of knowledge is doing, and it can hardly surprise that the triumph of this discipline falls into the 20th century when skepticism regarding the epistemological issue became dominant. Nevertheless, it is obvious that sociology of knowledge and epistemology are quite independent disciplines. At least this is true with regard to an alleged dependance of epistemology on the sociology of knowledge. Whoever rejects the naturalistic fallacy and accepts the impossibility to deduce normative propositions from descriptive ones, will have to recognize that the demonstration of social interests backing an epistemic system does not contribute anything to its verification or falsification and in general to its validation. The inverse relation, on the other side, is more complex. For sociology of knowledge claiming to be a science, it is subjected to epistemological analysis and criticism.

From what I have said it follows that also philosophy can be analysed in a double way. On the one hand, there is an epistemological analysis of philosophy —which, however, is insofar different from that of the other disciplines, as epistemology is itself a part, if not the core of philosophy. While the metatheory of chemistry is not chemistry, but philosophy, the metatheory of philosophy is and remains philosophy —for what else should the so-called metaphilosophy be than the essence of philosophy, at least if we understand metaphilosophy as epistemological discipline? The situation changes, if metaphilosophy is understood as that part of sociology of knowledge that deals with philosophy —this is in fact the alternative approach to philosophy. In fact one can understand the term "philosophy" as referring to two different entities. On the one hand, philosophy is an epistemic enterprise which has to satisfy certain normative criteria; on the other hand, philosophy is the part of our social system which claims to deal with philosophy in the first sense and is acknowleged by a significant number of persons to do so. Of course, the two entities are connected; the social subsystem called "philosophy" would destroy itself if it would give up the pretension to be linked with philosophy in the normative sense, and such a pretension is rarely utterly illusory. But despite all connections, they are two different things; it is neither an empirical nor an analytical truth that the social subsystem is really philosophy in the first sense. Well-paid professors of philosophy may have little to do with what philosophy is all about; and substantial philosophy may be done by persons who do not belong to the subsystem named "philosophy".[4]

After this clarification I can come back to the subject of my lecture. The clarification was necessary because my thesis is that the laws determining the selection of informations in the social subsystem are partly in contradiction with the needs of philosophy in the normative sense. Before I explain the normative concept of philosophy, let me name several traits of the modern way to practise philosophy and science. First, activities belonging to the epistemic system are based on remuneration. This seems obvious, but is not so. Great philosophers and scientists of the past, from Plato to Descartes and Schopenhauer, were often wealthy and regarded their research as something they owed to themselves and to nobody else. Important reasons for the collapse of the earlier social condition are the universalist belief that acquired wealth is more moral than inherited wealth, the increase of needs of modern man who does not like to live the often ascetic life of the great philosophers of the past, finally the growing number of persons active in the epistemic sector who could not all live from inherited wealth. At the beginning of modernity the state understood that it was in its interest to finance the universities and research institutes (particularly in the natural sciences). With the growth of state supported research in the humanities and in philosophy, the tradition of private sponsoring has faded away, at least in continental Europe, or it has become strongly interconnected with the university system via the review process; an aristocracy with good intellectual taste does not exist any longer, and entrepreneurs prefer to sponsor sports than philosophy. Thus a respectable life as a philosopher depends more and more on a career at a university. Furthermore, philosophical publications often presuppose funds; and the access to such publication organs —journals, book series etc.— is mainly controlled by professors teaching at universities. And even if someone succeeds in publishing a philosophical bestseller on the free market, it will be hardly acknowledged as good philosophy, because of a strong prejudice in favor of the universities as the center of the intellectual life. Such a prejudice did not exist in the 17th century when almost no important philosopher was integrated into a university; and it is likely that it will

4 B. GRÄFRATH has recently shown the difficulties brilliant outsiders have in the social subsystem called "philosophy" in his remarkable book: *Ketzer, Dilettanten und Genies. Grenzgänger der Philosophie*, Hamburg (Junius), 1993.

collapse again in the next century. Already now it is recognized by everybody that not every professor of philosophy is a philosopher in the normative sense of the word; soon also the inversion will be accepted —but not yet. What are the dangers of this new socio-economic situation? The high degree of intellectual autonomy which characterized many philosophers of the past has diminished in modern time with its increasing interdependence of the members of civil society and the egalitarian tendencies of mass democracy. Less and less philosophy professors dare to speak up their own mind without first having tried to find out how their colleagues think. The attention one dedicates to the sensibilities of one's colleagues is much higher than in the past; the amount of informations exchanged with sincere interest at every philosophical conference is usually by far larger, when it comes to questions of personal policy than during the discussion of the real subjects of philosophy.

This has partly to do with the second important aspect of the sociology of the modern epistemic systems: The number of the persons who work in them has dramatically increased, and thus the amount of information regarding one's own colleagues. The industrial revolution has set free more and more persons from physical labour, some of whom were real talents who in the past had no chance whatsoever to begin an academic career. But not all of them. The expansion of the universities in the 1960es in Germany, e.g., had to take in a large number of unqualified persons who now are there and take part in the decisions on the cooptation of the system, causing a continuous fall of the intellectual level —for it is a natural law of human psychology that mediocrity is afraid of what is better than itself. Whoever applies for a position has to count with them; and this means: He or she should read, or at least quote, their works. A large part of the activity of modern professors consists in reading and reviewing works of colleagues which are not always inspiring, also because the "publish or perish"-maxim of contemporary academia and the irreasonably large number of conferences forces to write also when one has not really something important to say. The number of the students is a further factor which determines significantly the informational environment of a modern philosophy professor, not to speak of the bureaucratization of the universities and the expansion of the power of the administration. Since, finally, criteria of success are the number of persons working at one's own institute as well as the amount of money one gets for his research project, the paper work increases.

When finally one has got, due to a good position, a certain personal autonomy and learned to manage the information flood related to students and administration, the contemporary books and papers one can read are characterized by a peculiar trait —they deal usually with very special issues. Specialisation is indeed the fate of all the sciences in the modern world. Why? One important reason for the specialization process is the above mentioned quantitative increase: This makes it possible that scholars dedicate their energy to relatively minor subjects that in former times were neglected, because more general ones had to be studied first by the scientific community. But specialization is not only a possibility, it is a necessary consequence of the social conditions of academia. As long as the academic system asks for "originality" (whatever it may be) already early in the career, a young philosopher will prefer to write an essay on a very minor and detailed question than to continue to study the principles of the different spheres of philosophy in order to achieve, perhaps, after many years a really original synthesis on a higher level of abstraction and of significance. Long-term projects are not frequent in our time, patience is a virtue that has become rare. The specialization process takes place in philosophy as well as in the other sciences. Therefore there are less and less scientists able to teach the philosopher what the principles of their own science are. The clarity the great physicists of the first half of this century had with regard to the scope, the aim and the grounds of their enterprise is missed in many of their successors. If someone wants to reflect philosophically on the principles of the social world, he will have to go back to books as Tönnies' *Gemeinschaft und Gesellschaft* or Weber's *Wirtschaft und Gesellschaft* in order to find an accurate analysis of the fundamental categories of sociology. More recent attempts to give a global view of one's own discipline, focusing on the essential issues, do scarcely exist. The study of another discipline besides philosophy rarely helps to develop a sense for principles —at least as these disciplines are taught nowadays.

I have intentionally chosen an example from the social sciences. For the social sciences have become one of the most powerful rivals of philosophy, often with the pretension to replace it altogether. My own statements till this point of my lecture have been more sociological than philosophical, and in fact in the beginning I recognized the complementarity of the sociological and the epistemological approaches to epistemic systems. Nowadays this complementarity is more and more given up in favor of the sociological point of view. On the one hand this is surprising, for the arguments for a superiority of the epistemological analysis are strong. On the other hand, the triumph of the empirical method in the natural sciences has suggested that only descriptive propositions are valid, and more and more philosophers try to compete with the empirical sciences by giving up any normative pretension. They try to ape the social, sometimes the natural sciences in a way which helps neither philosophy nor the empirical sciences. A considerable amount of philosophical literature today deals with the alleged end of philosophy, and many philosophers would have chosen to become something else if they had foreseen as students the ultimate skepticism to which they would come.

Another type of flight into objectivity is the study of the history of philosophy at the expense of philosophy itself. Also this has become a highly specialized enterprise; there are less and less persons who know the whole of the history of philosophy in a degree sufficient to answer such questions as whether there are tendencies of development, a progress towards certain insights etc. And there are even less persons who are both innovative philosophers and sufficiently familiar with the history of philosophy. The division between analytical and hermeneutical philosophy is to a great degree caused by the emancipation of philosophy and history of philosophy from each other.

III. The Normative Idea of Philosophy

It will probably not be denied that my description of the informational environment a modern philosopher has to deal with is fair. But why should we complain about this situation? Since I suggested before that the actual state of the social subsystem philosophy endangers its normative concept, I have to explain what philosophy in the normative sense is. How does it relate to the other sciences?[5] The first trait which belongs to philosophy in the more than social sense is its universality. Philosophy does not deal with a particular branch of being as, e.g., chemistry or art history: The aim of philosophy is the search for the whole. From its beginning till at least

5 I am influenced in the following analysis by Fichte's *Über den Begriff der Wissenschaftslehre*.

German idealism this has been one of the essential properties of philosophy most philosophers have acknowledged. And even if one regards this property as possible only in a time in which the differentiation of the sciences had not yet taken place, one has to concede that at least this is a characteristic trait of a philosophical insight that it has important consequences for all the other sciences. If, e.g., Wittgenstein's arguments against private language were true, our understanding of every science would change —be it mathematics, physics or history. There has been no great philosopher who has not given impulses to different sciences. This depends on the second important property of philosophy: It deals with the principles of the sciences. This is partly a consequence of the incapacity of philosophy to study all the knowable subjects, of its necessary self-limitation. More important, however, is the incapacity of the sciences to analyse themselves. In fact every demonstration in a science presupposes axioms from which the theorems can be deduced according to certain rules of demonstration; but the axioms and the rules are not justified within the science itself —they are simply presupposed without any reflexion. Reflexion on these presuppositions is peculiar of philosophy —on the rules of logic, on the material principles of the material branches of philosophy (e.g., on the concept of matter of the philosophy of nature). Here, however, a problem arises which brings in a third property of philosophy. Where do the principles of philosophy come from? I have already alluded to this issue speaking of epistemology; and indeed it seems to me that only that epistemology can be accepted that justifies itself and its own propositions. Reflexivity is therefore a central property of the epistemic system philosophy, and the prohibition of reflexivity which may make sense in some particular sciences destroys the essence of philosophy. (It goes without saying that foundational reflexivity has to be distinguished from the circling around oneself which is so typical of the contemporary social subsystem.) Fourth, philosophy is —at least to a large amount— a normative, not a descriptive discipline. Not the *quaestio facti*, the *quaestio iuris* is its domain; and therefore epistemology and ethics will always be parts of philosophy and never be reduced to sociology of knowledge or of mores. At least we must say: The act of such a reduction would always be a philosophical one; a skeptical result with regard to the justification problem might justify the reduction, but such a result and such a justification would still be an epistemological operation (very probably a self-defeating one). I do not claim that every branch of philosophy is normative —philosophy of nature is certainly not—; but where normative questions arise we can be sure that we are debating a philosophical issue. From the aforementioned properties of philosophy a fifth one follows with regard to its history —it is not linear. For linear progress can exist only within a paradigm, when certain presuppositions are accepted —philosophy, however, as a reflexion about the presuppositions of all knowledge and of itself is in a continuous paradigm crisis, and therefore philosophy cannot know progress in the same degree as, e.g., physics.[6] Sixth, philosophy presupposes even more than the other sciences a personal quality rarely found —courage, i.e. the disposition to question the convictions of one's own time and of one's own peer group without fear of social sanctions.

It is clear that an epistemic system with the named properties is not fostered by the social conditions analysed above which are in strident contradiction with philosophy's destination. This is particularly evident with regard to the first characteristic of philosophy, the search for the whole. Greek philosophers as Plato and Aristotle could still possess almost all knowledge of their time and even be creative in the different scientific disciplines —Plato in mathematics, Aristotle in biology. Without any hesitation Aristotle writes that the wise man ought to know all; and even if he adds: "as far it is possible and not knowing it in the particulars"[7], his sentence sounds almost ridiculous for a time like ours. The last philosopher who could claim to have contributed to almost all sciences is Leibniz; the last thinker who at least understood the essential results of the various disciplines of his time is Hegel. After him nobody has been able to grasp even the basics of all existing disciplines. Now, this could imply that we should reject philosophy and let the heritage of it be pursued by the natural and social sciences. A lot of epistemic systems have been given up in the history of mankind —why not finally also philosophy? The answer to this question is that philosophy is indeed an inevitable presupposition of the search for knowledge. In fact the crisis of philosophy has important consequences for the concept of knowledge itself. For the ancient belief in the intrinsic value of every unit of knowledge was rooted in the assumption that knowledge would converge to a unitary picture of a unitary world. Therefore the traditional idea of knowledge culminated in the concept of philosophy as that discipline which guaranteed the unity of knowledge. It makes sense to

---

6 See my analysis of the logic of the history of philosophy in: *Wahrheit und Geschichte*, Stuttgart-Bad Cannstatt (Frommann-Holzboog), 1984.

7 *Metaphysics* A 2, 982 a 8ff.

assume that one reason for the lack of enthusiasm with which scientific knowledge nowadays is acquired is the collapse of philosophy as ultimate reference point which alone could bestow on knowledge the glamour of an enterprise not only useful, but nobilitated by an intrinsic value. The sciences, the daughters of philosophy, by their emancipation and by the development of an alternative and seemingly successful model of knowledge seem to have overcome philosophy. But their victory will be a Pyrrhic one: By negating philosophy, they are sawing the branch on which they are sitting.

There is no alternative to the epistemic subsystem called philosophy, if knowledge shall be; and there are good philosophical arguments that the imperative that knowledge ought to be is a categorical one —for every argument against it presupposes the intrinsic value of knowledge which it tries to deny. Therefore one has to revitalize the normative concept of philosophy. But how? Illusory is the attempt to unify in one person the knowledge of all sciences. It is, however, still possible, although extremely difficult, to study the principles and methods of different sciences. As Plato said of the dialectician[8], a philosopher should be able to develop a synopsis of different fields. Philosophers should break out from the ivory tower of their discipline and seek the discussion with different sciences. One can even believe that it does make little sense to study only philosophy; one should come to philosophical questions through the analysis of the problems intrinsic to the single sciences. Obviously the philosopher needs the intellectual exchange with those scientists who are able to work out the essential features of their epistemic enterprise and are more interested in questions of a certain universality than in their own discoveries. Instead of running after the last numbers of academic journals, the philosopher ought to dedicate much energy to the study of well-grounded, general theories. To understand the theory of relativity is much more important for an epistemologist than to study the still frail attempts of a theory of elementary particles. Since often earlier theories are easier to grasp, but can teach certain features of the method practiced by a science as well, and sometimes even better than later ones, it is advisable to study the classics of the sciences —the study of Euclid does not replace that of Hilbert, but it is still a good introduction into mathematical philosophy.

Familiarity with the methods and results of different sciences may be necessary, it is certainly not a sufficient condition for good philosophy. For

8 *Republic* 537 c 7.

philosophy is both less and more than the sum of the other sciences —it has its own method and its own questions. Logic as the discipline how we ought to think is of fundamental importance for the study of philosophy. However, I would insist that logic must be conceived in a broader sense than is usually done. Not only formal logic, also what since Kant has been called transcendental logic belongs to logic in the full sense of the word. What transcendental arguments in their different variants are, is a central topic of philosophy, the study of this field a primary task for those interested in the autonomy of philosophy and its irreducibility to other sciences. Transcendental arguments can help to grasp the normative sphere; they are important both for theoretical and for practical philosophy. In mathematics it is not sufficient to have learned a formula, one has to apply it in order to internalize it. So in philosophy the training in transcendental arguments is what really matters.

But besides logic and rudimentary knowledge of the sciences the philosopher needs an eye for the structure of the phenomena. One cannot study only written books; the book of the world must be the ultimate authority. Nobody can become an originary philosopher without profound, often painful personal experiences. Certain truths must be lived in order that the argumentative intelligence be motivated to justify them. The phenomenological eye is often schooled by the study of great art; therefore art is a powerful source of inspiration for philosophy. One further thing philosophy can learn from art is the sense for the priority of the whole with regard to the parts. From the Greeks onward art works have been compared with organisms, and aptly so; for in a good work of art it is the idea of the whole which determines the structure of the single parts. The same is true with the most complex philosophical work, the system. Every system is based in an originary intuition of the whole which is then articulated step by step —while it is a sign of a weak philosophy when single propositions are developed without any awareness of their place in the whole of knowledge, of their significance for other branches of philosophy. Even worse is the situation when a philosopher's opinions are not even compatible with each other —when, e.g., his ethical convictions are in contradiction with his ontological assumptions. The best possible philosophy will be both simple and rich —it will explain many phenomena and at the same time be based on few and reasonable assumptions. If, however, one has to choose between two philosophies, one of which is phenomenologically rich and self-contradictory, the other poor and coherent, the second has to be preferred.

Because of the peculiar nature of philosophy, there is, as we have already noted, no linear progress in its history. Therefore past texts have an importance which is not matched by the significance of the classics in the other sciences. A modern physicist can not learn much from Aristotle's *Physics*, a philosopher of nature will. Thus a large amount of energy has to be dedicated to the reading of the main works of the great thinkers, possibly from different cultures. To have stated this, against the forgetfulness of the past in the analytical tradition, is a great merit of hermeneutical philosophy.[9] But the study of the classics can lead to substantial philosophy only if it is done with a primary concern for the validity of the arguments and the coherence of the systems of the philosophers, if we want to learn from them, not about them. The merely historical interest with which the classics are studied by the majority of the historians of philosophy will not inspire systematic philosophy, and philosophy students are led astray if they are obliged to spend much time with texts which are not yet felt to answer their own systematic questions. To give an example: One should read Sextus not in order to learn something about Hellenistic philosophy, but to understand argumentative strategies and logical problems of every skeptical theory. Since the study of the history of philosophy can show that the amount of possible philosophical systems is quite limited, it is certainly not only impossible, but also superfluous to read all classics. It is, however, reasonable to study representants of the different types of philosophy. In a time in which philosophy has more and more the task to create a common ground on which the different cultures may communicate, it is furthermore advisable to dedicate more time to extraeuropean philosophy than was done in the past.

But can the knowledge which good philosophers ought to aim at really be mastered? No; but this does not mean that it is not a reasonable regulative idea. We can approximate it only if we ignore most other informations which try to capture our attention. The mountains of secondary literature on the history of philosophy ought to be neglected; only those works which throw real light on the classics can be read with good conscience. —With regard to modern systematic books which have not yet been passed the test of the past one must develop an instinct in order to feel, after reading some pages of a book, whether it pays off to continue. The level of abstraction it maintains,

---

9 See H.-G. GADAMER's classic work *Wahrheit und Methode*, Tübingen (J.C.B. Mohr [Paul Siebeck]) 1960.

the literature it quotes, the style, the density of informations, the structure of the whole as visible from the content table are all relevant parameters. Nevertheless such an instinct is always fallible; and since it is not possible to get all new philosophical books in one's hands, works of genius may indeed escape one's attention. But the risk not to read an important book is much less than to lose time in reading many volumes from which one cannot learn anything relevant. —The category of marginal interest is essential for the economy not only of material, but also of intellectual goods. After having written a thorough work, e.g., on Wittgenstein there is a diminishing marginal interest in every new essay one might publish about him; and whoever has a global vision of philosophy, will change the subject and reject invitations to conferences on authors whom he knows sufficiently well. —These three maxims will not create only friends in academia; this is an ulterior advantage of them. The limitation of social contacts to the number of those persons from whom one can really learn something is strongly recommendable. For contacts not only take time: The habitude of loneliness is a necessary condition for creative thoughts. One can become free from prejudices only if one does not hear them every day. The use of organs which consist to a large degree of the repetition of commonplaces as newspapers etc. should be radically limited in order to hold the mind open. Ascetism has been rightly regarded by many thinkers of the past as a necessary condition for philosophy. Our consumerist age has poisoned all ascetic traditions with the known consequences for the environment, for the relations between developed and developing countries etc., and it is not difficult to see that without a renaissance of ascetic values the problems just named cannot be solved. The type of ascetism I am alone concerned with today in the name of philosophy can be called: informational ascetism.

Chapter 6

"Ethics of Journalism" or On Ethical Problems in the Mass Media

HARUN TEPE

The mass media are among the social institutions most frequently mentioned in our time. Rapidly advancing electronic technology, the resultant satellite broadcasts that nullify the significance of international borders, TV and radio transmissions for which walls constitute no obstacle —they all combine to make the press and media in general a highly important institution, one whose current power is undebatable.

I. The Need for a Mass Media Ethics

Together with the acquisition of power by the press have come increasing complaints about this power and the use to which it is put. As with all centers of power, the media have been and are being used for varying purposes, which are characterized as "good" and "bad". Thus the media are a source of both hope and fear, sometimes simultaneously, but at any rate are highly influential; and although this may vary from country to country according to the level of economic, political and technological development, the number of societies which are untouched by this influence is steadily dwindling. And while, depending on a country's political and economic order, different segments of society may benefit from this power, the fact remains that almost everywhere it does constitute a power. Correspondingly, one notes that in almost every society there are reactions to and complaints about the inevitable problems which arise from this power's abuse.

In our time there has consequently been mention of moral questions in the press and broadcasting, and of the need for a "journalistic morality" or "communication ethics". The idea is generally accepted that such a "morality" or journalistic ethics is necessary for journalists working in broadcasting or the press; but it is difficult to say that there is such a consensus over what this ethics might be, or ought to be. In order to secure ethical behavior on the part of their members, various press associations, and the press councils of some countries, have worked up professional codes and devised sanctions in an attempt to impose them on the parties concerned. What those who develop such a professional code actually try to do is attempt to put forward norms concerning what is and is not permissible for their members. In addition there are those who view the subject from a more theoretical framework, in terms of philosophy or philosophical ethics. But their numbers are not great; for as with other professional ethics, those who concern themselves with the ethics of journalism are mostly not philosophers but journalists and communications scientists. Philosophers tend to follow these developments from the sidelines, and although there are ever more of them dealing with the subject, they are still in the minority among those involved with mass media ethics. This paper is, then, the result of a perception of this lack.

Like medical ethics or bioethics, business ethics and environmental ethics, media ethics is one of the most frequently discussed ethics in our time. Indeed, professional ethics are not restricted to these four, for in a number of professions whose practitioners are aware of ethical questions there is mention of an ethics applicable to that field. For example librarians speak of a library ethics, research and educational scientists of a science ethics, and those who earn their living by commerce of a commerce ethics. Ultimately there are as many ethics, or at least such an expectation, as there are professions to demand them. The apparent lack of ethics is replaced by an "inflation" of professional ethics.

But as more "ethics" have emerged the concept of ethics has lost in clarity, and there is confusion over what can be expected from ethics as a branch of philosophy. This confusion has paved the way first for relativism in ethics, and then pluralism. Indeed, bolstered by certain currently fashionable schools of thought, there has been a strengthening and proliferation of the view that this relativism and pluralism are precisely what is desirable. This is because falsely based expectations give the impression that ethics in our day is faced with problems which it is unable to solve.

This paper will attempt to look from a philosophical viewpoint at the field denominated variously as "media ethics", "communication ethics", "journalistic ethics", etc., in various of its aspects, from the question of what this field should be called to certain of its problems. Its point of departure will be certain present-day views of ethics, as a major branch of philosophy; as well as certain anthropological views.

The paper will restrict itselt to a discussion of ethical problems encountered specifically in the mass media; but in a debate on media ethics many points may emerge which can shed light as well on current general ethical problems.

II. Professional "Ethics" in General and Mass Media Ethics

Discussion of ethical problems in the area of press and broadcasting makes reference to such headings as "media ethics", "press and broadcasting ethics", "communications ethics", "journalistic ethics" and the like. The designation varies partly, but not entirely, according to who requires such an ethic. Sometimes the focus is on an institution, at other times on journalists; sometimes it is on the ethical problems confronted by the reporter who converts events into news, at other times on the ethical problems of press or broadcasting organs, administrative organs, or the executives who head them.[1] Whatever the focus and the designation which results, in the end there is reference to a specific profession and an "ethic"

1 Comp. M. HALLER: "Die Journalisten und der Ethikbedarf", in: M. HALLER and H. HOLZHEY (Eds.): *Medien-Ethik: Beschreibungen, Analysen, Konzepte für den deutschsprachigen Journalismus*, Opladen (Westdeutscher Verlag) 1991, p. 196: "While as an individual the journalist is on the one hand presented as an extraordinary actor who can take the initiative,...on the other hand he is described as one who cannot take responsibility for his actions and is thus a mere cog in the giant media machinery".

proper to it and its practitioners. In this sense there is not a great deal to differentiate between the designations given above; nor does any great problem arise from the fact that various designations are assigned.

The problem is that, based on certain "ethical" questions that it encounters, each profession speaks of an ethics proper to itself; in other words, that by each profession adding the word ethics to its name —as with "science ethics", "business ethics" and "medical ethics"— the impression is created that there are as many "ethics" as professions, with the result that many think there are numerous ethics which differ in kind, sight thereby being lost of the common ground in ethical knowledge. Looking at "media ethics", or more precisely at the ethical problems of the press and broadcasting, one may ask: What kind of ethical problems are encountered in this field? Why is mention made of a "media" ethics? What kind of knowledge is expected from such an "ethics", and for whom?

Actually, the answer to these questions is not different from that elicited by the questions "what is ethics?", "why is the need felt for such a branch of knowledge?", "what kind of knowledge is ethical knowledge?" and "what does ethics provide the knowledge of?" Generally the answers given relevant to ethics, as a branch of philosophy, are the very answers given to the questions just listed. To quote Hermann Boventer,

> Since Aristotle, Ethics has been the philosophical discipline through which, in his words, 'we become good people'. My subject here is journalistic ethics, where the point is not to produce good people but good journalists.[2]

In short, if ethics provides knowledge that will contribute to producing "good people", journalistic ethics must provide knowledge that will help produce "good journalists". But what sort of contributions can ethics make to produce these "good" journalists? Indeed, who is a "good" journalist? In the article of which an excerpt has just been given Boventer does not answer this question, but he does mention such a journalist by name. He is Carl von Ossietzky, who as secretary of the German Peace Society ran a "No to New Wars" campaign after World War I, was awarded the Nobel Peace Prize in

2 H. BOVENTER: "Wertorientierter Journalismus. Die Sicht der Moralphilosophie", in: L. ERBRINGE ET AL (Ed.): *Medien Ohne Moral*, Berlin (Argon Verlag) 1988, p. 226.

1935, accepted it despite Nazi pressure to the contrary, and paid with his life after his arrest in 1938. What has been written about him confirms that Ossietzky was a journalist who to fight the Nazi regime put his life on the line and ended by losing it; but what led to the loss of his life was not his journalism but his character. Indeed, in this article by Boventer it is character which is exalted, the very quality which makes Ossietzky worthy of mention as an example. But this example does not shed much light on the question of what makes a "good journalist".

In another book[3] Boventer attempts to define a good journalist, that is to say, what is right (or wrong), good (or bad), for a journalist to do; and using these questions, he strives to make an introduction to ethical thinking and action in journalism. Whether or not he succeeds in this particular instance, it is clear that such a discussion which leads to ethical thinking and action, and which points up the need therefore, would be helpful in illuminating ethical problems in the field of journalism. For this is precisely what is needed: opening the way to "ethical thinking and action". But how, and by what means, is this to be achieved? To what degree can it be achieved with the professional codes or norms of behavior —and sometimes of evaluation— which today are generally what one expects from a professional ethics?

III. Ethical Problems of the Mass Media

Before answering the above-mentioned questions it is necessary to determine what sort of ethical problems are encountered in the press, and what kind of ethical approach to them might be useful in trying to solve them. If journalism is "gathering, selecting and processing topical information from differing social systems (circles), and offering them up again for use by these social systems",[4] then the actions of a journalist which involve ethical problems must be "gathering topical information",

---

3 H. BOVENTER: *Pressefreiheit ist nicht grenzlos: Einführung in die Medienethik*, Bonn (Bouvier) 1989, p. 13.

4 Cited by M. HALLER from S. Weischenberg and U. Hyenztsch: "Die Journalisten und der Ethikbedarf", in: M. HALLER and H. HOLZHEY (Eds.): *op. cit.*, pp. 196-197.

"selecting" it, processing it and offering it up.[5] Considering, as we do here, journalism to be restricted to news reporting, that is, leaving aside that journalism of radio and television which aims at entertaining,[6] the task undertaken by news journalism is to convert events into news and present them to the public, to inform members of the public about events which do not happen in their immediate vicinity. But contrary to what some journalists and communications scientists suppose, this job cannot be fully comprised under such headings as "gathering", "selecting", "processing" and "presentation". Not only do the activities so designated overlap, but each of them alone is connected with a number of problems. Is news something that is gathered? And does the journalist gather it, or produce it? Or is news generated by other means? What is news, and what place is occupied in it by the person who converts events into news? What are the ethical problems which may be involved in the latter activity?

1. Ethical Problems of the Reporter as "Newsmaker"

Based on this or that criterion, the "newsmaking" journalist selects one occurence from those going on around him and converts it into news. The result is that out of many occurences only one is chosen, made an "event", and presented to the public. The remaining occurences are relegated to the past, and so long as they are not noted and documented by someone else become fleeting moments in history, over with and forgotten. In short, every event becomes one thanks to someone who makes it so. He or she is the one who frames the event —but not, of course, the occurrence— starts and finishes it at a particular time. Thus in every event —in the process of its selection and presentation out of what occurs— there is a covert evaluation.[7]

5 *Ibid.*, p. 197.

6 Actually, there is no clear consensus about what activities count as journalism, and it is open to debate whether the producers of programs aimed strictly at entertainment should be considered journalists. But although, as with Haller, journalism is generally thought of as news reporting, these other types of activity are also thought of as journalism. (M. HALLER: *Ibid.*, pp. 196-197)

7 See: I. KUÇURADI: "Miscelanea on 'Ethics and Contemporary Journalism'", in: G. BÜKEN ET AL. (Ed.): *Emel Doğramacı'ya Armağan*, Ankara (Hacettepe University) 1998, p. 17.

In each "event" there is an inevitable perspective stemming from the person who has framed the event, for it becomes an "event" only through that person.[8] What the journalist will select from the unbroken flow of occurences, how he will define its limits, what point he will direct his gaze or camera toward —all depend on his capacity to see and evaluate and on what he wants to do, that is, on his goal. "Thus the possibility of taking different cross-sections of the same event gives rise to the possibility of making somewhat differing but nevertheless right interpretations".[9] But this does not mean that every interpretation, everything said about an event, will be correct. Even when the knowledge of that event is correct, it means that correctness here always has an element of perspectivity.[10]

A good number of the problems confronted in journalism are related to this point. In order to properly fulfill his function as a mediator, the journalist must be able to relate events correctly, to see them as they are without imputing or ascribing value to them.[11] Those of whom this is

---

8 Comp. I. KUÇURADI: *Insan ve Değerleri*, Istanbul (Yankı Yayınları) 1971, pp. 65-66: "When it is a question of evaluating events and situations... what we are offered is a portion of historical reality. And the evaluation of an event or situation emerges as an *interpretation* of that event or situation. The interpretation of historical reality supplies us with knowledge of an utterly different kind from that which one encounters in the history of philosophy... This knowledge, which might be called perspectived knowledge, arises from evaluations related to historical existence: from explanations and the interpretation of events and situations".

9 *Ibid.*, p. 66.

10 I. KUÇURADI: "Miscelanea on 'Ethics and Contemporary Journalism'", in: G. BÜKEN ET AL. (Ed.): *op. cit.*, p. 18: "This unavoidable perspectivity in framing an event bears implications for its evaluation; but it has, nevertheless, to be distinguished from what is often understood [by] 'perspectivity' —i.e. from the explanation of an event by means of existing different theories or by different analogies based on past experience— as well as to be distinguished from value imputations and value ascriptions to events (all of which also have a direct effect on our decisions)."

11 For the different modes of evaluation see: *Ibid.*, p. 15: "One mode of evaluating we observe is what I call *to impute value* to an individual object ... in accordance with a general value judgement or norm, valid for the evaluator.... Another mode or way of evaluating is what I call *to ascribe value* to the evaluated object —to an action, event, situation, etc.— with regard to a special connection which the evaluator sees between himself or herself and

expected are individual persons; and at the heart of an individual's ability to make right evaluations lies his or her intellectual equipment and fund of knowledge – ultimately, his or her capacities. Ethical training can develop these capacities, showing the possibility, for which various types of knowledge are required, of evaluating an event or situation, and indicating also the way in which this can be done. Contrary to what is usually expected from professional ethics, philosophical training does not offer a prescription for what must be done, or avoided, in each isolated circumstance or in given types of situation. Perhaps, as with a number of professional ethics, principles or norms of evaluation and action can be set forth which indicate how members of that profession should behave in given situations. Individuals can also be forced to abide by these norms; but this brings about neither right evaluation nor ethical action, for each situation experienced by the individual —here the journalist— even if it bears resemblances to other situations, is singular, that is, happens only once. Experienced at a particular time and place, it is over and done with. Thus, as with all other professional codes, that devised for the press deals with what should generally be done or avoided, and is inadequate in and of itself to enable right evaluation.

Looking at an event for no other reason than to bring about the goals of journalism, that is to convey what happens in literal terms to other people, the journalist must be able not only to grasp the event with his or her own eyes. He/She must treat the event in its singularity.[12] And the first step in this act is to frame the event —a framing which may vary with the framer. This is the first step in making an evaluation. "Only after it is framed can an event be explained, i.e. put in connection with other events, decisions etc. which constitute its main causes; and only then can it be put, if it is a past event, in connection with other events or situations which are its

---

the action, event, or situation in question, or with regard to a contingent result it bears for him or her."

12 This should not be confused with what Anton Hügli characterizes as "situation-based morality" (*Situationsmoral*) in drawing the distinction between that and "principle-based morality" (*Prinzipienmoral*) (A. HÜGLI: "Was haben die Medien mit Ethik zu tun?", in: M. HALLER and H. HOLZHEY (Eds.): *op. cit.*, pp. 61-62.) Here the necessity of dealing with each situation or event in its singularity does not prevent one from generalizing about this class of evaluations. In that sense this need does not utterly exclude Hüglis' "principle-based morality", that is, the act of making explanations based on principle.

consequences, and in the case of an event that is going on at the moment of its consideration, with its immediate and most probable consequences. But to see the ethical problems in an event necessitates the connection of its different main consequences —both real and highly probable consequences— with value knowledge".[13]

The problems considered so far have to do with journalistic activities labelled "gathering" and "selecting".[14] The "processing" of news, meanwhile, is an activity which, although it may also lead to certain other ethical problems, essentially faces the journalist with the types of ethical problems encountered in the "conversion of an event into news" discussed above. Therefore in the following section, before discussing "the processing of news", we shall consider the "presentation" of news and the problems which it entails.

2. Ethical Problems of Those Who Decide on Publishing News

The presentation of news on radio or television, or in the papers, and deciding which items among those which come to the editorial desk will be presented, and how, has been viewed by most communications scientists as an operation distinct from the "gathering" and "selection" of news. For this reason separate ethics have sometimes been proposed for the newsmaking journalist and his or her editor.[15] When the door opens on the room in which the prime minister has committed suicide, the cameraman may consult an ethic of intention (*Gesinnungethik*) in deciding what to do; while in printing or rejecting these images the guideline should be a publishing responsibility

---

13 I. KUÇURADI: "Miscelanea on 'Ethics and Contemporary Journalism'", in: G. BÜKEN ET AL (Ed.): *op. cit.*, p. 17.

14 As can be clearly understood from what is written above, these two activities are in no wise separate from one another, every act of gathering necessitating a selection; nor is "conversion into news" an act of "gathering". The journalist takes a cross-section from the infinite chain of occurrences, and then attempts to evaluate and convey this cross-section.

15 For this see P. VON ZAHN: "Zum 'Ethik-Bedarf' des Journalisten in hochindustrialisierten Gesellschaften", or, although the thrust is somewhat different, U. SAXER: "Journalistische Ethik im elektronischen Zeitalter – eine Chimare?", in: L. ERBRING ET AL (Ed.): *op. cit.*, pp. 21 and 278.

(*Verantwortungsethik*).[16] So goes the argument,[17] according to which the journalist, at the very tip of the news web, can decide according to an ethic of intention how he or she will act in a situation that arises —that is, can make decisions based on principle, as in Kantian ethics. On the other hand, say the adherents of this view, principled action will be insufficient for an editor or broadcast director, who must take responsibility for the foreseeable consequences of that action. His action affects not just himslef, but also a wide readership or audience; and therefore, it is said, the ethic appropriate for his or her case is one not of intention but of responsibility. H. Jonas in particular has noted that in our day there has been a marked increase in humankind's technical capabilities, so that one person's actions have a great impact on his/her surroundings as well as on him/herself, and therefore a new categorical imperative is needed[18]; and thanks to such remarks "responsibility" has become a fundamental category in ethical discussion.

---

16 The point of departure here is Max Weber's distinction between ethics or intention and ethics of responsibility, one which I find highly problematical (see M. WEBER: "Der Beruf zur Politik", in: *Soziologie, Universal-geschichtliche Analysen, Politik*, Stuttgart (Alfred Kröner) 1973, p. 174-175). Characterizing Kant's ethic as one of intention, Weber maintains that it proves inadequate for certain actions and should be complemented by an ethic of responsibility. Weber says that an ethic of intention refers to a maxim or fundamental principle in evaluating the rightness of an action, while an ethic of responsibility envisages the assumption of responsibility by the actor for the foreseeable results of his/her action. In short, whereas the ethic of intention is deontological in nature, the ethic of responsibility is teleological, being based not on the principle or intention which underlies an action but rather on its outcome.

17 Here the author is alluding to Uwe Barschel, president of the state of Schleswig-Holstein, who committed suicide after a political scandal that arose during an election campaign and was found dead in a hotel room by a journalist on November 11, 1987. Despite the shock he experienced on opening the door and seeing a dead body, the journalist, Sebastian Knauer, managed to take photos, which were widely published. Knauer was sharply criticized for this in the press, his actions being deemed "a scandal within a scandal" (P. VON ZAHN: "Zum 'Ethik-Bedarf' des Journalisten in hochindustrialisierten Gesellschaften", in: L. ERBRING ET AL (Ed.): *op. cit.*, p. 21).

18 For this see H. JONAS: *Das Prinzip Verantwortung. Versuch einer Ethik der technologische Zivilisation*, Frankfurt am Main, (Suhrkamp) 1984, esp. pp. 26-58.

Partly due to Jonas's influence, it is maintained that for the director of a nuclear energy plant, or a military officer who can decide whether or not to use the chemical weapons at his command, the important thing is not an ethic of intention; that what matters here is for the person in question to be cognizant of the catastrophic results which can stem from the technololgy at his/her disposal, to think of all the people who might be affected, and to act responsibly based on this awareness.[19] Similarly, says the argument, when an editor or broadcast director prints or broadcasts material, he must decide based on a consideration of all the people whom that material will impact; and this is not an ethic of intention but of responsibility.

The ethical problems encountered by those who must decide on whether or not to publish or broadcast a news item may, clearly, differ from the problems of the reporter or cameraman who brings it to the newsdesk. The jobs are different, so naturally the ensuing ethical problems may be as well. What the editor evaluates is not the same as what is evaluated by the reporter or cameraman. The latter select a "newsworthy" event or events from the chain of occurences, so what they evaluate are occurences; what the editor or program director has for evalution, on the other hand, are news items manufactured from events. Thus he or she is not directly confronted with occurences or persons. He/She is, however, directly confronted by news footage or texts, and must decide what to publish or broadcast, and how. In doing so, he/she will bear in mind the entire readership or audience of the potential news story, and also consider their expectations. His/Her decision may be entirely swayed by these expectations, or only slightly, as other factors, such as pressure from the media bosses or other circles, may play a greater role; and the editor or director may come to his/her own decision without considering all influences. But in every case, when the editor, director or producer allows a news item to be published or broadcast in a given way, he/she, to make an evaluation upon which to base his/her action, takes account of the material to hand, the target audience, and the potential impact of the broadcast.[20] As with the reporter or cameraman, the problem

---

19 KLEINSTEUBER, H.: "Neue Medien- Neue Technik- Neue Moral?", in: M. HALLER and H. HOLZHEY (Eds.): *Medien-Ethik: Beschreibungen, Analysen, Konzepte für den deutschsprachigen Journalismus*, Opladen (Westdeutscher Verlag) 1991, p. 313.

20 In 1991 the German Press Agency (DPA) was reported to receive roughly 500,000 words of material per day, of which some 50,000, or one-tenth, were sent to subscribers, while only a small portion of the latter number actually

here is one of evaluation. Like the journalist who converts an event into news,[21] those who must decide which event to report to the public and how —what relevant points will be stressed, what forms of expression used, what images and sound mix— also face a problem of right evaluation. In both cases, from the reporter at the tip of the communications web to the broadcast director who must give the final decision on printing or transmitting the news, each stage involves human beings, so that it is always persons who must decide, and correctly, implying that these decisions entail ethical responsibility. In all situations where the decision-maker is the person himself, or when the decision is shaped by the person himself, that person is responsible for the decision and for the action he/she takes or avoids because of it. In short, be it the actions of a reporter or cameraman, those of a program director, or those of any of us in our daily dealings, the problem is always one of "right evaluation".

This in turn, although there may be differences based on what is evaluated, at heart is a knowledge-based activity for which all cases structurally have something in common, requiring knowledge of differing types —factual knowledge per the thing being evaluated, and also value knowledge. For example "the right evaluation of a given action of a given person in given conditions follows formally three main steps: 1. The first step is understanding this action, which means to grasp, in as detailed a way as possible, a) the evaluation underlying this action itself, b) the value experience following it and c) the intention and aim of that action, as well as

ended up being published in newspapers or bracts on radio and TV (M. BUCHWALD: "Ist Ethik eine journalistische Handlungsmaxime?", in: M. HALLER and H. HOLZHEY (Eds.): *Medien-Ethik: Beschreibungen, Analysen, Konzepte für den deutschsprachigen Journalismus*, Opladen (Westdeutscher Verlag) 1991, p. 180). It is highly probable that the volume of news has increased since then.

21 The packaging of the event, the language used to convey it, and even the background music which accompanies the image, all may provide clues as to how the event is evaluated by that press or broadcasting organ, by those who prepare it and present it. Each new day brings examples of how the same event can be presented differently by different newspapers and television companies. This could hardly be otherwise when events are evaluated thoughtlessly by those who, not using their own eyes but bringing certain ready-made value judgements —evaluation norms— to bear, impute value to events and situations.

how these were carried out. 2) The second step of evaluating an action is to be able to see the *specificity of this action with regard to other possibilities of acting* in the conditions in which it was carried out or not.... This specificity of an action constitutes its value —the value of that given action—, which also determines its ethical value (its being a right or wrong action, valuable or valueless action). 3. But to be able to grasp this ethical value of an action, one further step is needed: to relate this possibility, actualized in the given conditions, to the knowledge of what we call human dignity —for example to the clear knowledge of the relevant human rights".[22]

Only if the steps described above can be taken, and the person making the evaluation possesses the requisite knowledge and vision at each step, only then may it be possible to make a right evaluation. This applies to the reporter as well as the editor or producer, even though what they evaluate differs. Indeed, the situation is the same not only for journalists but for members of all professions. Whatever is being evaluated, right evaluation is achieved via the above steps —provided, of course, that we do not wish to impute or ascribe value to the thing being evaluated.

IV. The Function of a Journalistic Code

In that case, what is to be expected from a "professional ethic" such as "media ethics"? What will be the function, in making right evaluation, of journalistic codes developed for members of the press?

Media ethics, or rather what might be expected from ethics in the solution by members of the press of the ethical problems they encounter, is help in gaining the awareness to see and illuminate the ethical problems inherent in events; and that ethical training might help enable them to do this, or develop in that direction. This in turn can be accomplished by imparting knowledge about ethical relationships, actions, evaluations, value and values, in the meantime generating discussion of ethical problems in the press sector to spark ethical awareness. Ethics cannot, however, go beyond this to provide

22 I. KUÇURADI: "Miscelanea on 'Ethics and Contemporary Journalism'", in: G. BÜKEN ET AL (Ed.): *op. cit.*, pp. 16-17.

a set of evaluative and behavioral norms which would be valid in each individual situation; nor can it establish norms for how to act or not act in given situations. At most it can tell us what it means to make evaluations using such ready-made norms, and show what it is the source from which these norms are derived.

For this reason it cannot be expected of ethics to develop journalistic codes which will tell journalists how to act in given situations. But one may look at these codes through the prism of philosophical knowledge and say of them the following: Such evaluative and behavioral norms cannot be applied by rote to specific types of situation to yield right evaluation, and if that should happen to be the outcome it is sheer coincidence.

What, then, is the function of such codes? Let us conclude by answering this question with the remarks of I. Kuçuradi, whose views on values and ethics[23] have provided the underpinning for this article:

"What is, then, the use of moral professional codes? They are useful in case a member of a profession, in our case a journalist, is unable, for any reason (objective or subjective), to make a right evaluation and to find out in a given situation what he or she must do in order to exercise the profession in accordance with its "what for". In such a case —and there are many such cases —a journalist, by applying a properly deduced general professional norm, may increase the probability —and only the probability— of protecting the right to correct information, or any other valuable objective; but this does not preclude the possibility that in that concrete individual case he gives damage to a valuable objective. For such cases professional moral codes are necessary; but perhaps they are necessary not so much because of these cases, but because there are many irresponsible members in each profession".[24]

---

23 I. KUÇURADI: *İnsan ve Değerleri*, Istanbul (Yankı Yayınları) 1971 and I. KUÇURADI: *Etik*, Ankara (Türkiye Felsefe Kurumu Yayınları) 1995.

24 I. KUÇURADI: "Miscelanea on 'Ethics and Contemporary Journalism'", in: G. BÜKEN ET AL (Ed.): *op. cit.*, p. 18.

Part Four

Ethical Problems in Law and Politics

Chapter 7

The Ethical Foundations of the Rule of Law

ZEYNEP DAVRAN

I. Introduction

In 1984 the Turkish Law Association granted its first Award of Honor to Hıfzı Veldet Velidedeoğlu, a professor of civil law, in recognition of his life-long crusade to uphold and to establish the rule of law. The award ceremony was attended by a select audience consisting of members of high courts, university professors and lawyers. Professor Muammer Aksoy, President of the Association, in his opening speech gave an intentionally non-academic definition of the rule of law in words which, in retrospect, read like a tragic prophecy:

> The rule of law prevails in a civil community when owing to the existence and enforcement of legal norms individuals can live in peace, sleep in peace and are not insecure about their future. In order to ensure that citizens do not live in constant fear of being deprived of their lives, liberties, properties and other rights on false accusations and unfounded charges of those in government or of those wielding power, certain rules have to be recognized as the basis of the political and legal order. The mere existence of a constitution preventing the concentration of political power in one person or body does not guarantee the protection of the above mentioned rights.

> Where the courts having both the power and duty to punish the offenders and grant remedial relief to the victims are subject to direct or indirect pressures from those holding political power, no one can live without a gnawing suspicion that his/her basic rights are in peril. Therefore, unless the courts are independent and the judges are protected against government interference the rule of law is an illusion. Again, where those accused have not been granted the right to defend themselves before courts and administrative bodies, there is no peace, no rule of law. To continue, where the penal laws are applied retroactively, ... where court hearings are not open to the public, ... where individuals are denied the basic rights and freedoms which are sometimes colorfully referred to as 'fortresses even governments are not permitted to enter' or 'government-free zones' are not recognized and where, in particular, life and personal integrity are not respected, ... if there is torture for whatever reason, there is no peace, no rule of law".[1]

Professor Aksoy, who considered, inter alia, living without fear of losing one's life as a result of unfounded accusations as one of the criteria of the rule of law, was a few years later killed in front of his apartment house by bullets fired into his head. Many of us have the persistent uneasy feeling that the authorities have not been doing the best they can to identify the assassins and bring them to justice.

II. The Relationship Between Law and Morality

If the rule of law as characterized in the above passage, which I have translated somewhat freely, presupposes and connotes elements such as the sanctity of human life, inviolability of a person's integrity, and protection of property against infringements by political authority, then it is evident that essentially the rule of law rests on moral principles, or that there is at least an overlap between the rule of law and morality, ergo, between morality and

---

1 M. AKSOY: *Hukuk Devleti ve Velidedeoğlu*, Istanbul (Çağdaş Yayınları) 1985, pp. 16-17.

law. Maybe the relationship is more than just a convergence of the two and I venture to say that unless legal norms conform to or are derived from ethical precepts, they will not be 'good' laws and will not be conducive to the supremacy of law. The 'perpetual unneasy feeling' referred to above actually means 'moral indignation' —moral indignation directed at the senseless murder of an intellectual of high caliber, of an honest innocent citizen. Another conclusion I draw from the 'non-academic' definition cited above is that the rule of law presupposes an ethical system which gives the individual a special status. The human being has a value, a dignity, an essential worth as expressed in Article I of the Universal Declaration of Human Rights: "All human beings are born free and equal in dignity and rights. They are endowed with reason and conscience and should act towards one another in the spirit of brotherhood".

What is more, concepts like 'justice', 'duty', 'obligation', 'right' etc. partake of both realms —morality and law. In fact, there is another sphere which cannot, which ought not, be divorced from them: politics. It is no wonder that Plato's *Republic*, his mature work on ethics, ontology, epistemology, aesthetics etc., starts with a search for the relationship between individuals and ends up with the proclamation that unless philosophers become kings or kings philosophers the ideal state will not be instituted. Aristotle, in the last sentences of *Nicomachean Ethics* says:

> Now our predecessors have left the subject of legislation to us unexamined, it is perhaps best therefore that we should ourselves study it, and in studying the question of the constitution, in order to complete to the best of our ability our *philosophy of human nature...* when these have been studied we shall perhaps be more likely to see with a comprehensive view, which constitution is best, and how each must be ordered and what *laws* and *customs* it must use, if it is to be at its best...[2]

What Aristotle seems to be saying is that understanding human nature and customs (we have to keep in mind that 'custom' and 'ethics' come from the same root) and laws is necessary for the constitution of the best form of government.. Although the identification of metaphysics, epistemology,

2 ARISTOTLE: *Ethica Nicomachea*, in: The Basic Works of Aristotle translated by V.D. Ross, New York (Random House. Edited by Richard McKeon).

ethics and politics we observe in the Platonic system is not found in Aristotle's politics, he points out to the relatedness of certain areas of human nature (psychology?), ethics, laws and political organizations. And, in the common-sense view, we in fact believe that there are, and ought to be, moral criteria for assessing the 'goodness' of a legal system.

Admittedly, the difficulty here is to identify and delineate what ultimate values we accept in making an ethical evaluation of law in general and of the rule of law in particular. In determining these values, scientific processes (such as sociological studies and statistics) and analytical thinking are important. Through empirical investigations we can determine which moral values are in fact accepted in a particular society at a given time, but the most rigorous scientific method cannot make ultimate choices for one person or for a group of persons, nor can it verify the choices made. In the final analysis these choices depend to a great extent on the individual's own world-view, how he sees the place of man, his place in the universe and in society. In a more philosophically technical sense, we must have recourse to a more or less *foundationalist* view that systems of belief are justified by virtue of the logical relations that obtain between beliefs which require justification and other beliefs which themselves are in no need of justification. A foundationalist approach to capital punishment would run somewhat like the following: 'A' believes capital punishment is wrong, taking this to follow from the self-evident principle that it is wrong to kill people and his belief that 'B' is a person. Incidentally, this is Locke's method in his *Treatises* when he starts with 'life, liberty, property' as givens and to those of his critics of who claim there is a contradiction between his epistemology, which is empirical (all knowledge starts from experience), and his ethics I might venture to answer that at least methodologically there is no inconsistency —he is a foundationalist in both areas.

So our basic beliefs about the value of man himself, of the individual as a creature of dignity and essential worth, values of liberty and equality, material requisites of a decent life, the opportunity for people to participate significantly in the control of their government —all point to the natural law theory as a viable basis also of law and the rule of law. It is my contention that natural law is a useful device to answer such questions as the grounds for the authority of the state, the rationale for respect and observance of the laws, the relationship between laws and morality (which comes first, which determines the other) and even the justification of civil disobedience. I am quite aware that natural law is a two-edged sword: one can justify opposing views by recourse to the explanatory construct which natural law is. Before going into natural law theory in some detail, let me state that the position I find congenial is a combination, a mixture, of the thought of Aristotle, Locke and the contemporary jurist Lon. L. Fuller, and not the line starting from Hobbes and extending to the legal positivists, via utilitarianism.

III. Natural Law Theories

The basic meaning of the rule of law is the most ancient Aristotle in his *Politics*, Book. III, Chap XIII says:

> He who commands that law should rule may thus be regarded as commanding that God and reason alone should rule; he who commands that a man should rule adds the character of the beast. Appetite has that character; and high spirit, too, perverts the holders of office, even when they are the best of men. Law [as the pure voice of God and reason] may thus be defined as "Reason free from all passion".

Aristotle's use of the word 'God' should not be taken in a theological sense, although it of course takes on this meaning in Aquinas, who was greatly influenced by him.

Greek thought expressed by Aristotle seeped into the main current of Western ideas about law and government primarily through the Roman Stoics who postulated a view of the universe, of man and of law. Cicero says:

> True law is right reason in agreement with nature; it is of universal application, unchanging and everlasting; it summons to duty by its commands, and averts from wrongdoing by its prohibitions... We cannot be freed from its obligations by senate or people, and we need not look outside ourselves for an expounder or interpreter of it. And there will not be different laws at Rome and at Athens, or different laws now and in the future, but one eternal and unchangeable law will be valid for all nations and all times, and there will be one master and

> ruler, that is, God, over us all, for he is the author of this law, its promulgator, and its enforcing judge...[3]

Christian thinking was based on these foundations and produced a theory of government and law which brought justice and authority together. The universal order, emanating from god's mind, is to a certain extent perceptible to man's rational faculties, and as natural law, provides a universal standard for human law by those invested with the care of the community. The aim of law and government is the common good.

With the Reformation the unity of medieval thought was ended and belief and confidence in a universal and knowable standard of justice waned. At the same time the emerging spirit of nationalism led to the founding of powerful states whose varying legislations constituted the justification and validation of positive law as the enactment of universal justice. The theory of territorial sovereignty was developed to explain and justify the law-making and law-enforcing aspirations of the new nation states. The most influential theorist of this movement was Thomas Hobbes. He expounded his views in the *Leviathan* published in 1651. Hobbes is a materialist and for him everything which exists is matter and everything that occurs is motion. He accounts for human behaviour in these limited terms. All mental states and behaviour, all motivation are explained in terms of motion. Desire is the result of attraction (pleasure) or repulsion (pain) between man and an external object. It is natural for him to seek self-preservation and that heightening of vital activity which he explains as pleasure while avoiding pain. In a solitary state man is 'nasty and brutish'. Uncontrolled egoistic and hedonic impulses make each man an enemy of every other, and even of himself when his desires make him imprudent. The original condition of man is thus a state of war in which there is neither justice or property nor any right except the minimal one of self-defence. Self-interest is not served at all by such a state of wretchedness, and man's reason leads him to peace through the establishment of government and the voluntary surrender to it of self-authority in areas where the desires of individuals are incompatible. Such surrender is conditional on the equal sacrifice of all and on the political effectiveness of the sovereign to enforce the agreement. Under no conditions, however, does anyone give up his right to self-preservation. Morality thus depends on the means and institutions by which peace is secured. Duty and obligation are relative to

---

3 *De Re Publica*, Book III, XXII.

socially enforceable laws; justice is relative to contracts insured by political sanctions. The 'good' never loses its basically subjective reference although repeated experiences lead us to regard as objective good and right what the commonwealth permits, since this is, in the long run, the most likely way of maximizing one's own pleasure. He sets up his commonwealth on the basis of a social contract.

The response to Hobbes was immediate and strong. Those who grounded morality and legality either in religion or reason were furious. There were critical appraisals which challenged his view of morality and later his notion of man —appraisals which resulted in constructive insights into the problems of ethics. The first important criticisms were focused on Hobbes' theory that morality is conventional, that legality makes right and illegality, wrong. Sudden defeat in war, slower changes in custom, or even the weakness of governments can thereby convert what is wrong today into a right tomorrow. On the whole, critics of Hobbes did not debate the priority of legal to ethical norms; they rather affirmed that morality is universal, permanent, and independent of specific social and political conditions. As a part of the anatomy of the world, morals are objective and knowledge about them is available to reason by methods not significantly different from those of the sciences, especially mathematics. Moreover, morality provides its own appeal and 'requiredness' as does logic. For instance, Cudworth makes an objection to Hobbes which takes the form of pointing out that to promise or make a contract, reference is needed to a prior morality, such acts require prior morality. Moral axioms are needed in the derivation of moral conclusions (we see the beginnings of the 'is-ought' controversy which later will be the main, the substantial point of difference between natural law thinkers and legal positivists). Cumberland held that moral laws were expressions of God's legislation, but on the whole, response to Hobbes did not rely on theological arguments. The Cambridge Platonists (Cudworth, Henry More, Samuel Clarke) were in general agreement that reason intuits moral realities, but they differ on the nature of this reality. They were committed to a deductively connected system of moral knowledge resting on a foundation of easily known and unquestionable moral truths serving as axioms. Their position reflected the epistemology of rationalism. With reservation about rationalism, especially in physics, we see reservation about rationalism in ethics.

John Locke is an empiricist and the Cambridge Platonists are rationalists, but they agreed on important issues in ethics. Locke believes that all sources of knowledge give information about objective moral truth, that morality derives from sensible experiences of pleasure and pain. Moral truths may also be demonstrated as mathematical ones, and his suggestion for moral axioms is the famous proposition that total liberty is impossible under government and that without property there is no justice. He claims that the universe is so designed that rewards and punishments, when coupled with pleasure and pain as motives, integrate private virtue and pleasure with the social good. Locke's *Two Treatises on Civil Government* was an apology for the Revolution of 1688. There he opposed a relativistic approach to morality. There were fundamental moral principles termed 'laws of nature' whose claim on men was not contingent on governmental sanctions, and the interpretation of which did not reside in the hands of any one individual.

Locke's position with regard to natural law is seen clearly in the following quotation from his *Second Treatise on Civil Government*:

> ... It is certain there is such a law, and that, too, as intelligible and plain to a rational creature and a studier of that law as the positive laws of commonwealths; nay, possibly plainer, as much as reason is easier to be understood than the fancies and intricate contrivances of men, following contrary and hidden interests put into words; for truly so are a great part of the municiple laws of countries, which are only so far right as they are founded on the law of nature, by which they are to be regulated and interpreted.[4]

These laws are considered by Locke to be self-evident, which means they are open to intuitive apperception, but only after sufficient demonstration. He claims that they may be deduced from a consideration of man with regard to our idea of God; and this may be demonstrated from the intuitive knowledge which we possess of our own existence. Can one provide an empirical interpretation for these laws of nature? For Hobbes, the laws of nature appear to function much like empirical hypotheses which have been gained through experience, and which are cited as the best possible means of achieving a particular end. Locke's laws have little about them of experiential nature. For instance, he claims that everyone is bound to preserve his own life because

---

4 From *An Essay Concerning the True Origin, Extent and End of Civil Government, Second Treatise on Civil Government*, as quoted in: SIR ERNEST BARKER: *Social Contract*, New York (Oxford University Press) 1967, p. 7.

God has made men to last during his own pleasure. He says very little concerning an empirical end when discussing the derivation of these rules. But yet in other places he asserts that good and evil are nothing but pleasure and pain, or that which occasions or produces pleasure and pain. Here he is providing a naturalistic interpretation for these terms, and he also maintains in the chapter entitled "The Idea of Power" in Book II of his *Essay Concerning Human Understanding*, that all men seek happiness (pleasure), and this would seem to establish it as a natural end for men. And in his *Second Treatise on Civil Government* he further asserts that law (which in this context also includes natural law) operates as a necessary condition for the attainment of natural right. Since men's natural rights include happiness (or pleasure) as has been stated above, and indeed as life, liberty and property may themselves be derived from pleasure in the form of necessary conditions for its attainment, it seems reasonable to assume that good may be considered to be an end towards which the laws of nature provide a necessary means. This interpretation of Locke, if accurate, would bring his conception of natural law into a closer juxtaposition with Hobbes' position than has usually been suspected.

But still, Locke's laws of nature do not present one with the picture of empirical extrapolations which have been ascertained by a process of experiment and trial and error. However, even admitting this, it is still not necessary to assume that they could not be subject to a demonstration which includes the idea of pleasure as a basic factor. For indeed, according to Locke's *Essay*, all discursive reasoning can take place only with ideas. And a demonstration consists in devising intermediate steps for a final intuitive grasp of certain ideas which are not immediately self-evident. Therefore, the idea of pleasure need not be excluded from an abstract demonstration of the laws of nature. There may have been two reasons for him to exclude the adoption of a utilitarian point of view: First because pleasure seeking is not unique to man. Second, while believing that his laws of nature do have a tendency to promote happiness, he did not believe that this was either the most unique or the most profitable justification for them.

To show that Locke held that natural law was demonstrable, as the Cambridge Platonists did, I quote the following passage from *An Essay Concerning Human Understanding* Book. IV, Chap. III:

> 'Where there is no property there is no injustice', is a proposition as certain as any demonstration in Euclid; for the idea of property being

(by definition) a right to anything, and the idea of which the name injustice is given being (by definition) an invasion or violation of that right, it is evident that these ideas, being thus established (by definitions), and these names annexed to them, I can as certainly know this proposition to be true as I know that a triangle has three angles equal to two right ones.[5]

IV. The Positivist Attack on Natural Law

David Hume's analysis of morality stems from his views on epistemology. The objects of human reason (what can be known) according to Hume, are divided into two distinct categories. First, there are relations of ideas which are intuitively or demonstratively certain (logic, mathematics). The second class includes matters of fact which are contingent. While the negation of propositions about relations of ideas leads to logical contradiction, so truths of relations of ideas are universal and necessary. The second class includes matters of fact (empirical truths) which are contingent, which means that the contrary of every matter of fact is possible, there are no observed necessary connections between matters of fact, the necessity lies solely in the mind and is a result of custom or habit. So the necessity involved in causation is only a psychological necessity.

Hume rejects reason as the source of moral distinctions just as he rejected reason as a justification for the causal inference. In addition, the source of moral distinctions will be found to lie in an internal sense just as the idea of a necessary connection arose from a feeling or sentiment of the mind. His attack against the role of reason in morality is directed against those philosophers who maintained that there are eternal and absolute moral values, "that there are immutable measures of right and wrong; that morality, like truth, is discerned merely by comparison". According to Hume, reason is wholly inactive and since morals have a great influence on actions the rules of morality cannot be derived from reason. However, moral sense is active rather than passive; reason, in the strictest sense, is concerned with relations of ideas. The four relations of ideas are resemblance, contrariety, degrees of

---

5 Parentheses mine.

quality, and proportions in quantity and number. Therefore, if morality consists of relations which are certain and demonstrable, they must consist of at least one of the four relations. But Hume goes on to argue that the rules of morality do not consist in these relations. Thus, just as reason was unable to give us the idea of necessary connections, reason is incapable of providing moral rules. Reason is inactive "whether it considers the powers of external bodies, or the actions of rational beings".

Hume maintains not only that morality doesn't consist in the relations of ideas, but that it does not consist in any matters of fact which can be discovered by the understanding. We never find virtue *in the object*, just as we never find causal powers in the object; we only find virtue and vice through an internal feeling. Granted that this is a matter of fact, nevertheless it is a matter of fact which is a matter of feeling and not of reason. It is an internal impression analogous to the internal feeling of a necessary connection. Moral distinctions, then, are not discovered merely by reason, they must be discovered by some internal sense. This Hume calls "the moral sense". Therefore, morality, as well as causality, is more a matter of feeling than of reason. If the boundaries of morality were determined by the understanding, they would be either relations of ideas or matters of fact. Let us suppose that a person is torn between two courses of action and that he wishes to decide which is right. Let us further suppose that he has access to all the knowledge of mathematics and logic as well as of all empirical matters. Then the question is: does he have at hand a principle which is sufficient, or even relevant, to determine which is the good alternative. Hume's answer is no. Reason can indicate the likely consequences of one choice or another and thereby direct the passions, but it does not recommend the beneficial consequences over the non-beneficial ones, nor alone provide the interest or attractiveness of either. Morality is more properly felt than judged of, for it is the nature of virtue to be amiable rather than true, and of vice to be odious rather than false.

Hume has made certain strong and disturbing points here. From the knowledge of what is the case, what is right can never be inferred. If an argument concludes with what *ought* to be the case, one of the premises must contain an ought; and this ought depends in the long run on some commitment which may utilize data supplied by reason but is itself non-cognitive. Furthermore, if there is no valid standard, then morality seems to be subjective and relative to each of us. Hume did not like this last consequence, therefore developed his ideas of sympathy, utility and the relation of morals to pleasure and approval. The pivotal point for our purposes is Hume's putting an unbridgeable gap between 'ought' and 'is' or norm and fact; this radical separation of the two realms was the starting point for legal positivism (actually, positivism in general). In the contemporary scene, positivism combined with linguistic analysis (for instance L. Wittgenstein's work on the uses of language as an answer to the puzzles or paradoxes that have haunted philosophers) pointed out the distinction between normative and factual uses of language. Thus, the following view came to be adopted by philosophers and legal theorists: a statement that something ought to be done is not intended to give a factual description but to prescribe a course of action based on the implication that reasons exist for so acting, and also on the standards of evaluation by which those reasons may be judged. A rule of law is different in that, although it does not state a fact but only prescribes a course of action, it does not necessarily imply that reasons for compliance could be sought and perhaps given, but rather that it is derived from a valid authority. It is only another norm which can be that authority (to cite just one example, this is Kelsen's line of thinking).

V. Conclusion

At the beginning of my paper I said that the rule of law rests on legal norms that conform to or are derived from ethical precepts. I further submit that those ethical precepts are true, that is, they are expressed in propositions that can be true.

John Finnis says:

> Natural law refers to the set of propositions picking out (1) basic human goods, (2) general requirements of right choosing, and (3) the specific moral norms deducible from those requirements as they bear on particular basic goods. A theory of natural law, or natural law theory is, therefore, a theory which argues that propositions of those

> three sorts can be *true* and offers to identify at least some of these propositions and their implications for theory and practice.[6]

One distinction has to be made. Natural law and theories of natural law are not the same things. Theories of natural law have a history, there have been revivals and eclipses; for instance, when positivism in philosophy is in vogue natural law theories are out, when there are gross injustices, crimes against humanity, they are back in again. On the other hand, if there are true principles and norms of natural law, they are true independently of any theories about them.

---

6 J. FINNIS (Ed.): *Natural Law*, Volume I., England (Dartmouth Publishing Company Ltd.) 1991, p. 24.

Chapter 8

Professional Ethics in Legislation and Adjudication in the Constitutional State

FRIEDRICH KÜBLER

I. Definition of the Issue

1. For the definition of the issue, four points of reference or corner points of the proposed topic ought to be addressed:

a) Firstly, it concerns a *professional code of ethics*, i.e. inquiries are made about function specific responsibilities, the rules of which are developed in a particular field of practical activity and are imparted and passed on further mainly through a specific form of professional socialization, for instance a particular training.

b) This code of ethics is applied to statutes and law. To deal with this material, a particular professional group has emerged —lawyers. Their origins lie in the late Middle Ages. On the European continent academic training to be a Doctor of Law, *doctor iuris*, came into being first of all in the law faculties of Upper Italy. The subject of the studies were the rediscovered texts of Roman Law. In the British Isles, the administration of justice was, above all, purely a teaching profession. The young students of law were trained in the practice of law by elder colleagues already in the practice. In the course of time this difference was smoothed away. The modern training of lawyers is composed almost universally of academic theoretical and at the same time of practical elements.

c) A third point, though, is that it is not a matter of a lawyers' universal professional code of ethics. I am asked to deal with the duties, specific to the profession, in the legislative institutions and the application of the law. That implies the further question concerning the difference between these two functions. The difference depends on what we understand the law to be. I shall come back to this point in a moment.

d) Finally, our deliberations ought to hold true only for the relationships in a constitutional State governed by law. By accepting that, the theme becomes historically restricted. The constitutional State governed by law is a product of Europe's modern age. It is based on the idea that all secular power is subject to the law. Thus the law becomes the definitive authority of modern societies. Wherever the rule of the constitutional State governed by law is accepted, social conflicts are basically to be mediated according to the rules of the law.

2. What we mean by the concept of "law" is of fundamental importance for further deliberations. This is true above all —but not solely— for the demarcation between legislation and the application of the law. The word "Law" has had very different meanings for different epochs in modern development. It is proposed to point out the differences between three historical periods.

a) For the constitutional State governed by law of the pre-liberal period, statutes were based on law that was not made by men, but was predetermined, had been handed down to them; this is the epoch of natural law.

b) For the liberal constitutional State, statutes rested on the "*volonté générale*", i.e. on the understanding and the recognition by all citizens marked out on the basis of property and education. The statutes appeared in the form of a comprehensive book of law, the codification.

c) Finally, in the democratic constitutional State, the statutes became the product of a political process concerned with conflicts and regulated by compromises, for which the majority principle holds good. The statutes become measures with which specific economic or social effects are supposed to be achieved.

In what follows the demands which are made on lawyers by the professional code of ethics in the context of this course of historical events are to be discussed. For this, it has to be made clear that it is a matter of simplifying the typical models of the pre-liberal, the liberal and the democratic constitutional State, whose elements frequently have the appearance of being all mixed up together. In other words, one is forced into simplifications, all of which give this paper the character of a wood-cut and not that of a map where pains have been taken with all the details.

II. The Epoch of the Pre-liberal State

1. It is the age of enlightened natural law. Statutes are the expression not of law made by men, but of law handed down to them by a superordinate authority. This law is part of a divine world order whose plan is accessible to human insight. The sources of this knowledge are various. The law can be based on revelation through a sacred text, by means of which a supernatural authority speaks to mankind. This applies to the Old and the New Testaments and likewise to the Koran. The law can also be understood as being vested in the physical composition of the world. That corresponds with the narrower concept of natural law. Finally, law can be viewed as an ordering of society that has been handed down as the major element of a *status quo* desired by God in this and no other form. This is true in particular for the *ius commune*, the common law of the continent or for the English common law. They are acknowledged and passed on as part of a preordained order.

2. What, then, is the role of a specific legal code of professional ethics in a world of this kind? What is crucial is that the law is based on predetermined and intelligible principles accessible to human intelligence. The reality of the law is existent and capable of being experienced. This reality is, admittedly, not always evident. It requires, much more, the individual effort, the cognitive exertion, which becomes an act of scientific knowledge as a consequence of an academic *socialisation.* The methodical approach depends, once again, on the character in which the supernatural disposition is taken to be predetermined. If it is the revealed text of the Holy Scriptures, as is the case for important parts of Protestantism, then its interpretation, the theological hermeneutic, allows access to the understanding of what men hold to be right. If, on the contrary, we find the divine creation plan in the legitimacy of the ways it conforms to surrounding nature, then the law develops from contemplating it in speculative reasoning. One example lies in the organicist theories of law, which are inferred from the constitution of mankind in the proper organisation of society and the norms which create it. Since to have a head is innate for mankind, which uses it to come to decisions, the polity has

need of a monarch, who as head co-ordinates the working of its limbs and organs. Where the recorded law, as *ius commune* or Common Law, delivers the normative guideline, the lawyers make use of their specific legal discipline, methods of interpretation, systemisation and cautious further development of the order handed down in the particular texts.

3. In doing this, the professional code of legal ethics of the epoch of enlightened natural law becomes tangible. It is a scientific professional code, supported by what is left of the stocks of religious tradition. As the heavily veiled material substance of the law is accessible to individual perception, it counts as one of the most important duties of lawyers to put themselves to every conceivable effort to achieve insight into the fixed structure of the law. In this the difference between legislation and its application plays at most a small part. The principle of the separation of powers has still not gained acceptance. Privy councils or cabinets attend to the tasks of legislators and, likewise, to those of judges. Both activities are similar; in the final analysis, it is a matter of insight into the preordained principles of proper order. Integration into the structure of a monarchical State is equally undamaging. The ruler, too, is subordinate to the divine order, to which he owes his office. In the transition from absolutism to enlightened monarchy, lawyers change from being servants of the monarch to becoming servants of the State. Their professional access to a perception of the true law characterizes the proficiency with which they do the required work in legislation and the administration of justice for the polity.

III. Radical Change in Professional Ethics Occasioned by the Transition to the Liberal State

1. This transformation has many causes. Of particular importance is the epistemological critique of the philosophical foundations of Natural Law. Kant, above all, proved that there is no sure way to derive from the existence of our physical surrounding generally binding rules, that is to say the material principles of a *ius naturale*. Thus the conclusion becomes inescapable that the law is not based on a divine arrangement, but is a human product. Admittedly this sets to one side the ruler's traditional ties to legal principles, which are laid down for him too. In order to make provision

against a retreat into absolutism, the liberal theory regarding law and the State develops the doctrine of the *"contrat social"* , the contract binding on all citizens, in which they agree on the fundaments of their collective existence. Its practical legal meaning probably is most clearly visible in Rousseau's doctrine of the *"volonté générale"*. This is the shared conviction of the common-sense and the correctness of the rules which determine the reciprocal relationship of individuals, by all those citizens who, because of their property and education, are called on to take part in public affairs. These norms no longer rest on a preordained order whose structure would be accessible to the insight of individuals. They are much more the result of an empirical and collective process of perception, which has to run through a series of institutionalised stages. Particularly important is the institution of public opinion. It forms a forum —by way of salons, interest groups, learned societies and the rapidly developing opinion-forming press— a forum, in which the problems of regulatory control of bourgeois society are openly debated without reservation until the will of the generality is manifested in a consensus. This agreement is formally recorded in the vote of a further institution, that of the parliament elected by the citizens. This vote sanctions the statute which henceforward is binding on all. It possesses certain characteristics distinguishing it from all its predecessors and successors. It gives evidence of the consensus as to regulations which can permanently determine reasonable human behaviour. It therefore presents itself as a regulation fixed and concluded once and for all, a comprehensive Statute Book. This ideal is reflected in the great codifications from the Code Napoléon, the German BGB (Civil Statutes Book), and the Swiss ZGB (Civil Statutes Book) to the Civil Statute Books of Turkey and Japan. It is a characteristic of all of them that they were passed unanimously after lengthy consultations in commissions and parliaments and that, with them, legislation was separated from the application of statutes by adjudication.

2. This development is confronted primarily with the question of the professional ethical implications of liberal legislation, in which lawyers had taken an unrivalled and outstanding part, in scholarly preparation as well as in parliamentary debates. There are several aspects here to be differentiated. Fundamental is, primarily, the declaration of belief in the convictions of the Enlightenment, especially in the discernment that law is a human product, for which society bears responsibility. In the second place there is a readiness for committed participation in the collective process of perception, which produces the *volonté générale* and thus codification. Public assent to the aims

of the works of the legislature counts towards this, for which in Germany Thibauth's defence of the ideals of the codification against the attacks by the romantic-conservative school has to be mentioned as a particularly impressive example. No less important is expert work on the details. This is primarily influenced by the historical reviewing of the valid foundations of law, in the rules of which, matured over centuries, there appears visible —admittedly not without exception but still frequently— evidence of a kind of practical usefulness. Something similar is true of the work in those commissions answerable for the elaboration and formulation of detail and, thus, responsible for a code of rules consistent within itself and free of contradictions. To be emphasised above all, however, is an unwavering aim at the goal of the public good, paired with a readiness to submit to the better argument and thus to make possible the unanimous approval of the grand design.

3. In the course of the legislative procedure there is no clear separation between judges, ministerial bureaucracy and professors. Members of court and ministerial advisory councils are frequently at the same time outstanding academics. Meanwhile, relationships develop quite differently where it is no longer a question of establishing the law but of judges applying it, between which two aspects the principle of the separation of powers demands a strictly observed division. Where the judge has to decide an individual case, he is no longer taking part in the collective procedure of ascertaining the *volonté générale*; the outcome of this process is determined by the statute passed by parliament. Therefore it has on its side the guarantee of the correctness of its content; the individual conviction of the single judge must not be elevated over the common perception, shared by all, in the rationality of the regulation concerned. Out of this emerges a perception of the judge's indispensable attachment to statutory law. This is a rule of law which is, after all, supported by professional ethics, which do not just forbid dishonest motivation, corruptibility, venality, prejudice and bias in an affair that concerns oneself, but are elementary provisos for any form of the rule of law. In a formulation by Montesquieu, the judge is restricted to being no more than "*la bouche de la loi*", the mouth of the law. That means that any recourse to his own beliefs as to the law is strictly forbidden. He has to apply the parliamentary statute to the letter even where it flagrantly and diametrically contradicts his own personal views of justice. There is no Natural Law that permits the legitimacy of the *volonté générale* to be attacked or even merely to be doubted. Where a judge becomes involved in an unbearable conflict with his conscience, there is nothing left for him but to

resign from his office. Where the statute book, contrary to plan, allows room for interpretation, the judicial doctrine of interpretation takes over the task of eliminating, through clearly defined rules of art, any discretion by the judge. The office of judge demands the knowledge and the minute observance not only of the statute but also of the rules of its interpretation.

IV. Renewed Changes in the Context and Function of Legal Professional Ethics as a Consequence of the Transition from a Liberal to a Democratic State

1. This change primarily alters legislation in a manner that is extraordinarily important for our topic:

a) The self-appraisal that bourgeois society is homogenous was taken as the basis of the liberal conception of the State and the Law. All individuals have the same interests, as far as actions by the State are concerned. The task of the State is to establish and maintain an order which gives room for freedom to everybody for economic and cultural self-development —a freedom that is limited basically, not by legal barriers, but by the needs of others to expand, i.e. limited by the market. In other words, all citizens have a fully congruent interest in the rules of law, which guarantee a lasting framework for the competition of enterprises and for the competition of ideas. This concept, on which the ideal of the great codifications rested, was shattered as a result of industrialisation. With the culturally rootless and socially increasingly dependent stratum of the workers, the proletariat, there evolved a rapidly growing social group, the improvement of whose situation was, at the very least, no longer to be achieved by the market alone, but primarily by changing the conditions of the legal framework. For this reason those dependent on wages joined together, firstly in trade unions and later in political parties, which put the liberal system in question and sought to replace it by a socialist or, at the very least, a social-democratic system. Other groups copied this self-organisation by the working class. From then on there emerged associations of industry, commerce, agriculture, etc., while simultaneously the spectrum of the political parties was altered. In the place of the loosely structured clubs of the liberal bourgeoisie came more or less strictly organised mass organisations, which differed from one another in the sharply contrasting aims of their programmes. In the early stage, the socio-cultural groups were to a wide extent identical with the parties. Only in the course of the 20th century did the larger integrated parties arise, with the aim of at least partially securing an internal settlement among conflicting interests.

b) This change affects not only the procedure of legislation but also the purpose and form of statutes. In the face of the profound ideological disagreements between the parties, there were and are no grounds for hoping for a consensus. In this way, bourgeois agreement as a basis for the validity of the law collapses, and in its place appears the dominance of the majority principle. Where no single party has the majority of votes at its disposal there arise more or less short-term coalitions of parties with some joint purposes, which then coalesce by way of mutual give and take over specific regulations. The law documents the compromise on which the groupings competing with one another have agreed. At the same time, this suggests a change in the function of the laws. They are, as a rule, no longer intended to create a framework of order, neutral as to the outcome, for the ups and downs of the market. Thenceforth, the course of the market is supposed to be corrected or driven to attain concrete economic or social objectives, which aim at mainly short-term effects and are then, on occasion, amended or repealed, whenever the coalition which produced them is replaced by another political constellation. This tendency is reinforced even more with the transition to federal systems, in which laws are enacted at several levels. A case in point is the European Union. Up to now, European legal harmonisation has meant that the Union regulates isolated points, in the form of directives, which are to be integrated into their respective law arrangements and to permeate these as though they were a European-wide law.

2. It is not hard to see that this change has radically altered the conditions which make it possible for us to speak of judicial professional ethics in the framework of the legislature. These difficulties are based on several circumstances, which are to be briefly clarified in the following way:

a) In the liberal constitutional State governed by law, legislation was a collective process of discovery methods, in the framework of which the jurist was summoned to scholarly collaboration. Above all, the detailed work on the great codifications was a matter for the legal experts. As a rule they had, in this, no political guidelines to follow, but they did have an understanding shaped by years of experience of the material and systematic research into the respective problem areas. Their code of ethics was that of academics called to follow their own sense of responsibility. In the process of democratic legislation the two roles separate. The objective stimuli, i.e. the arrangements which the new regulation is supposed to bring about are predetermined by the politicians, who are under the dictates of their respective constituencies since they are led by the understandable desire to be successful once more at the next election. First of all, proposals regarding new statutes are discussed within the party organisations; then follow agreements with coalition partners and only then does the detailed work of the parliamentary committees begin. For the lawyers it still amounts to the role of being mere attendants. It is their responsibility to indicate the problems in the system which the introduction of the new provisions will occasion in the structure of current law. The questions of implementing or pushing through the regulation which has to be passed are also numbered amongst these problems, and additionally they, the lawyers, have to assist in the formulation of the wording of the text. In carrying out this function, they have different and various taskmasters: an association, which represents quite particular interests, a party group, which employs them as aides, and above all the government, to which they, as established public servants in their respective ministries, are accountable in looking after the legislative procedure. Finally there is the possibility that they may be called upon to give political advice in the role of independent experts. In each of these cases there is an employer or contracting agent to whom loyalty is owed. The extent of these ties is in no way constant. It depends on the employer and the nature of the relationship with him. Whoever has dealings as a company lawyer or as an expert witness finds himself in a role similar to that of an attorney. In the intimate relationship with the client there certainly exists, to be sure, the obligation to warn and to point out the negative consequences which a project may have not just for the client but also for others. In the outward relationship, the dominant element is the representation of interests. The employer or contracting agent may expect that his interests be emphasised in the representations made, even where they do not conform with the individual views of the lawyers engaged in them. Whoever is unable to do this must withdraw from his contract. The established civil servant in a ministry has to adhere to a somewhat different role model. He is assuredly under obligations of obedience and loyalty to his minister and, thereby, to the government. He is not, however, an employee of the government party, but a servant of the state. Therefore, he is also duty bound to protect the interests of the public at large. Where important requirements of the general public are at stake, this means the duty involves internal contradictions, and it can be legitimate and advisable that the differing view to the outside world be represented. The role of legal political consultation can be seen in a yet another light. Here the advantages and disadvantages of the measures under examination are to be weighed against one another.

b) An additional difficulty arises from the fact that in many cases there is no binding procedure for the issue of public welfare that has just been addressed. This was otherwise within the liberal model, where the homogeneity of views and interests made possible an agreement by all, the outcome of which incorporated even the desires of the general public within a binding formula. The statutes as a product of the collective viewpoint had to be superior to the conviction of the individual every time. In a pluralistic democracy it is questionable whether there can indeed ever be a consensus of such a kind. What is certain is that none is necessarily reflected in the content of the statutes. The law is much more the expression of quite specified interests and perceptions. Anyone who has other interests or adheres to other convictions has every reason for considering the law to be bad. For the legitimacy of the law, it may only be adduced that, as the result of the play of political forces, it reflects the needs of the electorate more reliably than does an individual opinion, which again is wrapped up in ideas specific to a group. On closer examination, admittedly, there are further differences to take into account. Primarily, the constitution gives a framework which reflects the basic consensus of society, insofar as there may be said to be an obligation imposed by a code of professional ethics to work in a way not resulting in statutes which are clearly contrary to the constitution. For the actual field of law and politics, it is possible to discern a difference between statutes which raise the level of economic efficiency and those which are supposed to distribute the available goods differently. Distribution is a task that is primarily political and for which democratic sanction is indispensable. Efficiency can, within limits, be determined by economic analysis. In doing so, admittedly, it is not solely the lawyers that are sought after but also other disciplines of social science, particularly economics. This outcome assigns to the experts the professional ethical obligation to warn against efficiency-reducing laws that help nobody and harm everybody. Finally, especially for the lawyers, there is a particular responsibility to be assumed for the detailed legal technical work, which does not concern the political aim so much as the manner of its integration into the existing legal organisation. Here it is less a matter of conflicts of loyalty than competence in the matter and the care which is to be exercised.

3. A distinction is to be drawn between judges and lawyers in the application of the law. In the case of judges:

a) Once again one should start with a brief review of the liberal constitutional State. In it the Law was absolutely binding on the judge, because it corresponded to being an emanation of the *volonté générale* which defined the public good. The legislature was shrewder at any time than the judge. In the democratic constitutional State, too, judges are subordinate to the law. This relationship from now is based on other factors. Primarily, this constitutional principle of a democracy is decisive. The judge, who speaks in the name of democracy, has to take the will of the people into consideration. He abuses his duty if he fails to comply with the decision of the majority in order to follow his own convictions as to the law. At the same time, it is the constitutional State governed by law which demands judicial loyalty to its legislation, for the law is fundamentally there in the interest of those who are subordinate to it —that law, in which the requirement for legal organisation is embodied in a way which they can recognise. This legal norm, however, is as a rule no longer part of a comprehensive codification whose parts are meticulously co-ordinated with one another. It is often a matter of the measures already mentioned, which are taken by a specific political grouping to achieve specific distinct goals. This increasingly gives rise to problems of consistency. The statutes are no longer sufficiently co-ordinated with one another. Inconsistencies arise which can no longer be solved solely according to the principles that the later statute has precedence over the earlier and the particular over the general. As the process of legislation provides for only a limited capacity to effect this, the adjustment of old law to long changed circumstances is delayed. For a long time it has been evident that the legislature in such cases relies on the help of the judges. Then it becomes the task of the judge to make his contribution, by judicial correction of the norm, to the task of constantly adapting to altered circumstances statutory law which was drafted at short notice anyway. Every investigation of harmonising law shows very clearly that highly developed systems of law are unable to function without this form of further adaptive shaping by judges.

b) Thus, the judge's professional ethical commitment to duty becomes complicated in a manner that can be indicated only briefly here. It no longer allows him to withdraw to the traditional position of a strict commitment to duty. Lower courts have, in every case, to pay tribute to the findings of higher courts in the administration of justice and, as a rule, to follow them. All courts are called on to take pains to achieve consistency in the ordering of the law. This can mean that earlier laws have to adapt to changed circumstances. Even the revision of new laws can, however, be legitimate and advisable. This holds true to some extent where there have been obvious mistakes in the editing of the text. In all these cases, the question is posed as to the measures which the judge may invoke for a revision of statute law. Here it is appropriate to warn against having recourse to individual perceptions of what is moral. It is at the very least uncertain whether it can be compulsorily demanded of the legal community as a whole. A first normative orientation arises from the constitution. It acknowledges values, above all basic and human rights, which are binding in the same way for all citizens of a polity, and it regulates the procedures and jurisdictions of importance in generating law. It is precisely this aspect which is of importance. Even where a change in the law is clearly advisable, the judge must ask himself whether it lies within his competence to bring about the change or whether he ought not leave it to parliamentary legislative procedures. New statutes which have already executed a parallel adaptation of law offer further opportunities of material correction. Finally, even here the distinction already mentioned between efficiency policy and distribution policy can gain in importance. Revision of the law to remedy market failures is a traditional task of judges, to which also belong the creation of the obligation to inform and the obligation to prevent harm. Redistribution of available goods, on the other hand, is even here primarily a political task which must be left to the parliament elected by and answerable to the people. In summary, the professional code of a judge's ethics demands that he not fail in the task of judicially shaping the law, that in this he remain aware of the boundaries to be respected and that, when doing so, he follow not his own private perceptions of justice, but the normative yardsticks which he finds in the legal and constitutional structures.

4) It is fitting to close with some remarks concerning lawyers. There can be no doubt that that they, within the framework of what is allowed by law, are bound in duty primarily to the wishes and needs of their clients. The increasingly difficult question is how far, in addition, they have to take the interests of the public at large into consideration. In the law of the constitutional courts of the legal structures of continental Europe lawyers are often described as "organs of the administration of justice". This allocates to them a role that shows certain analogies to that of the judge. The lawyer of

the 18th and 19th Centuries in general corresponded to this image. As a respected member of the caste of bourgeois notabilities and as a colleague well-known and frequently also personally connected to the judges, he quite understood how to represent his clients without losing his detachment from them, on which his reputation in the courts rested. This image has changed more and more in the course of recent decades. The number of lawyers has shot up and with this the spectrum of attitudes to the profession has widened. What is certain is that the lawyer who embodies the traditional virtues of integrity, reliability, care for objectivity and detachment from the interests of his employer has in no way disappeared. Alongside him, though, increasingly there are new interpretations of the role of the profession to be found which are hard to reconcile with the tasks of an organ of the administration of justice. This manifests itself from time to time in political cases in which the defending counsel identifies himself, without restriction, with the extremist position of the accused and participates in his strategy to use the trial as an attack on the legitimacy of the court and the legal system. Another variation is the corporation lawyer, who becomes his client's partner and thus acts as an entrepreneur himself. In this examples the change from an organ for the administration of justice to a service industry is seen particularly clearly. A consequence of this development, which looms with ever-increasing clarity, is the transformation from unwritten rules of professional ethics into rules prescribed by statute. This development can be understood as a warning against expecting from the jurist's ethical code an improvement in the essence of the administration of justice. In spite of this, there are good reasons to assume that the survival of the kernel of the jurist's attachment to the code of professional ethics remains indispensable.

Chapter 9

The Rule of Law and the Judge

HAYRETTIN ÖKÇESIZ

I. Introduction

Law, although in the words of Immanuel Kant[1] we still do not know what it is, is related to practical philosophy in a direct, clear way. Thus the concepts of phiosophical ethics, professional ethics and professional ethos are subsumed in a quite undevious manner under "value", one of the three dimensions of law. In this aspect the law in any case is ethical in character.

The fourth sub-heading of our seminar program is "Ethics and Those Who Formulate and Apply Law under the Rule of Law"; and this immediately takes us away from legal ethics or legal philosophy in the above sense, and from discussion of the ethical value of norms, into the ethical and factual realm of Man, who is after all law's actor.

The topic of our session embraces the concept of the rule of law. From here we arrive by a spiral path at philosophies of the state, political and legal sociology, and above all at legal philosopy in the sense of legal methodology.

In this context the subject of this paper, "The Rule of Law and the Judge", is used as a framework to

(1) delineate the characterization of the judge postulated as a neutral and independent third person;

---

1 I. KANT: *Kritik der reinen Vernunft* 2, Werkausgabe Band IV, ed. by Wilhelm Weischedel, Frankfurt/M (Suhrkamp) 6th ed. 1982, p. 625: "Achieving it [definition] is lovely but generally very difficult. Jurists are still looking for a definition of their own legal concepts".

(2) explore the individual responsibility and accountability of the judge given the parallelism between the evolution of the rule of law and that of legal interpretation;

(3) sum up, in lieu of a conclusion, with a critical examination of the judge as he or she is confronted by what I see as the three touchstones of justiceship: freedom of thought, the death penalty and civil disobedience.

II. The Postulate of the Neutral and Independent Third Person

I would like to begin with two definitions of the law. The first is by Ralf Dreier: "Law is the sum total of norms belonging to the main body of a system of norms either constituted by the state or international in character. This system should, however, in general have a social effect and a minimal ethical legitimacy, or at least be perceived as having the latter. Law is at the same time the totality of norms set forth by this constitution; but they should have a minimal social effect or the chance of having such, and also a minimal ethical legitimacy or the capacity to be perceived as having such".[2]

The second definition is owing to Günter Dux: "Law is a group of norms whereby society does not leave the securing of its validities to those who have been harmed by their violation, and in pursuit of this aim most often itself takes organized measures".[3]

The profile of a judge which emerges from these two definitions is notable for its ethical and sociological dimensions: a neutral and independent third person possessing a minimum of ethical knowledge and awareness who, among other attributes, enables norms to have a social effect... Perhaps that is how the judge should be defined. As is implied by these remarks, the judge, as a philosophical, neutral and independent third person, is more than anything else a social postulate: a postulate which with these capacities resolves conflict, strife and discord, and to that aim is equally distant, or near, to all parties (essentially embodying the ethical value named equality); a postulate which would transform justice into a social entity.

2 R. DREIER: *Recht-Staat-Vernunft.* Studien zur Rechtstheorie 2, Frankfurt/M (Suhrkamp) 1991, p. 116.

3 G. DUX: *Rechtssoziologie*, Stuttgart (Kohlhammer) 1978, p. 131.

When this postulate began to be a utopia, or when it began to be realized that it was one, society bestirred itself anew and began to generate ideas and ideologies whose goal was to assure that the postulate would be a utopia no longer. First on the agenda was an arbiterless dispute. With a new law, legitimized by a new minimal morality, this third person once again began to be a reality. The judge is an important lever of society. So deeply rooted is the image of the judge in human thought and feeling that it is part of all versions of the sacred: God too is a judge. Authoring a book after his retirement, a member of the Turkish Supreme Court could not resist quoting a French colleague: "To judge a human being is a divine act".[4]

Viewed from whatever angle, a consensus that the legal system is just and the judge both neutral and independent cannot spare the fact of a class justice from scientific scrutiny. Diverging from such predecessors as K. Liebknecht, E. Frankel and O. Kahn Freund while refraining from a value judgement, H. Rottleuthner defines this unclothed emperor as follows: "Class justice is an application of the law guided by a predisposition which is warped to favor the objective interests of one or more classes".[5]

Rottleuthner uses this concept to explain how the possibilities of legal interpretation change places for class reasons, and also how closely, in certain areas, the application of the law is connected to the political system. Lautmann, on the other hand, maintains that social justice is a structural outcome of its own justice systems and of the manner in which social control operates.[6] Man desires that justice light up our night like the moon, but on its dark side there is a stain of political justice.

In his preface to Alexander von Brünneck's *Politische Justiz gegen Kommunisten in der Bundesrepublik Deutschland 1949-1968*, Erhard Denniger writes the following: "The concept of political justice underlying this work is taken very broadly, and stems from these well-known words of Otto Kirchheimer: 'one may speak of political justice when the processes in the form of judicial reasoning are used for political ends'. That a trial is political 'emerges when it is so placed as to be a direct factor in the political struggle'. In this sense it is not important whether the participants in the

---

4 Ç. AŞÇIOĞLU, "*Doğru ve Güvenli Yargılanma Hakkımız Var!*", Ankara, 2nd ed. 1995, p. 133.

5 R. LAUTMANN: "Klassenjustiz", in: A. GÖRLITZ (Ed.): *Handlexikon zur Rechtswissenschaft*, vol. 1, Hamburg (Rororo) 1974, p. 249.

6 *Ibid.*, p. 252.

trial subjectively be conscious of having 'an impact on the distribution of political power'. Even if such considerations as adherence to the law and equality before the law lead them to reject such a political function, the objective character of their activities remains unchanged. Political justice is not restricted to such felonies and treason or threatening national security, but also includes, when they bear on political conflict, cases related to constitutional law, administrative law, civil law and labor law. As the work before us demonstrates, political justice shades over into every branch of the law. The presentation deals particularly with administrative pressures, for administrative and judicial intervention can often be understood only through their mutual relationships. The mode of administrative treatment partially predetermines the application of the law".[7]

Revolutionary courts, people's courts, tribunals of independence, martial law courts, courts set up to deal with "extraordinary circumstances", the whole range of courts dealing with political cases in "ordinary circumstances": they cannot help but pass before our eyes like a reel of film, along with the trials and sessions, accused parties, prosecutors, judges, convicts and executioners that they featured.

Can an ethical course be plotted using the legal-sociological exposition given above? Can one speak of a body of ethical norms which ought to motivate the actions of a judge or a jurist in general; of a "legal ethic", a "judicial ethic" similar to this "political ethic"? What sort of course, what sort of code might this be?

III. The Judge Under the Rule of Law[8]

As is well known, the rule of law, while in terms of form and content harboring a historical development, today is in both respects the sine qua non of a democratic regime concerned with the welfare of its citizens; while a

7 A. VON BRÜNNECK, *Politische Justiz gegen Kommunisten in der Bundesrepublik Deutschland 1949-1968*, Frankfurt/M (Suhrkamp) 1978, p. 11 ff.

8 For these remarks on the rule of law see H. ÖKÇESIZ, "Hukuk Devleti Olgusu", in: H. ÖKÇESIZ (Ed.): *Hukuksal Olgular Araştırması ve Hukuk Devleti - Rechtstatsachenforschung und Rechtsstaat*, Istanbul (HFSA/3), p. 140 ff.

regime that is not democratic or welfare-oriented cannot be enjoying the rule of law as it is understood today. If a state is characterized by a) separation of powers, b) independence of the courts, c) respect of the government for law, d) a judicial process independent of the government, and e) a guarantee of compensation for injury incurred through government actions, then there is formally the rule of law. Constitutional rulings are one of the final stages of such a characterization. This structure is a successful model of the state thanks to which a bourgeois or civil society can fulfill to the maximum the individual's demands for life, liberty and the right to own property —a model which keeps the way open to the possibility of answering the needs of the new age. The concept of the rule of law appears as the slogan of a new class and society in its struggle against the state, which, along with government, would be restrained by law. Here the concept of law is markedly different from any that had gone before. In addition to generality and continuity there is another important feature ensuring the rule of law: that power derive unconditionally from the people. The fundamental rights and freedoms for which the revolution was fought, and which are its fruits, can never be abolished, and can be limited when necessary only by the people's own representatives. This activity of national assemblies is called law-making, and it is only this which can restrict the demands for life, liberty and the right to own property. Both the state and society are subject to the supremacy of such law; and another name for this principle is the rule of law. This expresses both the beginning and to a large degree today's situation. From the idea of natural law, and its application, we proceed to legal positivism, at the same time with a new concept of the state. The formal rule of law is tied to a positivistic idea of the law and of legislation. Law means that which guarantees the interests of the new class, and only that can be the source of obedience to it, and of its legitimacy. Meanwhile in legal interpretation this picture is completed by all the resources of conceptual jurisprudence. Here I believe it would be appropriate, in examining the rule of law, to also make use of Max Weber's analysis of capitalist society and the modern age.

The rationality of the new age's social structure first appears as legal positivism and the formal rule of law, both of which are logical outcomes of the concept of law and the state implied by Weber's formal rationality.

In this model laws are independent of certain ideas of binding natural law, with no necessary relationship existing between law and morality. Any type of content may be law, which here obviously means positive law. It is in this sense that one should understand the dictum "a law is a law". Kant, too, held morality to be distinct from legality.

If in Weber's view law is an order guaranteed by an apparatus of compulsion, then this new set of laws, equally valid and applicable to all, should be guaranteed by a compelling apparatus that fits this definition. A set of laws which safeguarded the liberty and property of the new third class, to which the state was unconditionally subject, and which in the meantime forbid any sort of moral demand would naturally be perceived as a necessary phenomenon of capitalism's formal rationality. The formal rule of law is nothing more nor less than the state which constitutes the compelling apparatus mentioned above.

A certain parallelism is observed in the 19th century development of the philosophy of law and the state, with Weber's treatment of the modern capitalist age. Law and the state are understood formally, while legal safeguards have priority, necessary consequences of formal rationalism and the rationalization of the new reality. Only capable of intellectual grasping and of control thanks to the conceiving of a rationality peculiar to itself, and to the realization of this in turn as the rationalization of social existence, the new reality has in recent times acquired a special dimension to a degree which cannot be explained through formal concepts of law and the state.

The recent large-scale disasters of the 20th century have shown that a formal-rationalistic perspective and world view is inadequate in certain respects. Signs of this need for completion are first seen in the general theory of law and the most recent definitions of law, of which a typical example is the one by R. Dreier given above. Here one finds an expression of the awareness that a positive norm lacking some minimal ethical content cannot be considered law. Parallel to social and political developments forcing the state to provide for the welfare of its citizens, this necessary minimal ethical content not only lends to the rule of law its formal aspect, but also leads to the material rule of law which provides it with value content. This distinction between a formal and a material rule of law, which I believe reflects formal-contentual rationality, does not, in my view, just because it is a product of socio-political development, constitute a return to Weber's rational schematic, while at a more advanced stage it is explicable as a value-charged rational act, as inviolable human dignity becomes a concept which embraces the protection of universal rights as the purpose of the state (e.g. the German Constitution, article 1/1 or the Turkish Constitution, article 2).

THE RULE OF LAW AND THE JUDGE

The rule of law as outlined above provides clues as to how the judge's function should be understood by him/herself and by society: just as it may be taken from the perspective of legal methodology, on a technical plane related to modes of professional interpretation, so too it can be viewed as a purely ethical matter related directly to the judge's character.

The most typical question implying ethical responsibility is the following: should a judge who does not find a given legal norm just apply it merely because of its positive character?

Starting with a rigid positivist approach ("a law is a law" or "any type of content may be a decree of law") growing out of a formal understanding of the rule of law, one sees methodology develop to give an ever milder praxis enriched by theories such as free law and the interpretation of values.[9]

This development of legal methodology runs parallel to that of the rule of law, and its first stage has several dimensions: the school of conceptual interpretation which, intoxicated by large-scale codifications divorced from social reality, and in the faith that the law could be seamless, attempted to build a pyramid of concepts to solve legal enigmas; the movement to prohibit interpretation, formulated through Montesquieu's assertion that a judge is merely the mouthpiece of the law; and the school of interest interpretation which until the pre-World War II era strove to fill the gap through subjective teleology, that is by seeking to ferret out and reconstitute the will of the historical legislator, but which gradually came to conceive of law's purposive element in an objective teleological fashion, that is in terms of the will of the present-day abstract legislator. It is after this point that commence the legal methodologies of the contemporary philosophy of the rule of law.

In any potential conflict or competition among the three fundamental values of the idea of law[10] —justice, conformity to purpose, and the security of the law— a judge must choose one of these possible approaches to

9 For example, "In the search for criteria governing "new" decisions [those that create law], the interpretation of objective values does not merely refer the jurist to the law, but indicates there is a case for invoking personal judgement. Referring to the "objective spirit (*Geist*)" implies an array of criteria independent of him/her who is doing the judging", H.-M. PAWLOWSKI: *Methodenlehre für Juristen*, Heidelberg, Karlsruhe (C.F. Müller) 1981, p. 74.

10 For the pertinent Radbruch/Kaufmann schematic of the idea of law see H. ÖKÇESIZ: *Sivil Itaatsizlik*, Istanbul (AFA) 1994, p. 102.

interpretation. That is to say, he or she must personally decide when, and for what reasons, an expansive, or, conversely, restrictive interpretation is called for; and put that decision on a permanent footing. In our day the judge, too, is condemned to freedom, a freedom which ends his or her status as an automaton of decisions to give him/her immense responsibility vis-à-vis others.

In one sense Article 1 of the Turkish Civil Code (and the Swiss Civil Code) can provide a significant contribution as a rule for interpretation. Although it was thought for a time that it made possible the implementation of Free Law,[11] it in fact has a technical application in a narrow zone between the interpretation of concepts and the interpretation of interests. This article opens the way rather to a positivist reading of the law; or an insufficient degree of meaning has been gained for it to dissuade jurists from this conviction. Developments relative to this article have borne out the maxim that the only thing that the law cannot generate its own interpretation.[12] Like the defining of the law by a law, this is an utterly impossible task.[13] The ability and power of the judge to create, and by implication to interpret, the law arises outside any legal code.

What is the approach to interpretation that takes the judge even beyond the intention of the everyday legislator? Does the modern idea of law permit the creation of law by some new legislator who would replace the traditional and extant one? To phrase the former question differently: the principle that without law there can be no crime or punishment —*nullum crimen sine lege, nulla poena sine lege*— was a great gain for the rule of law. Would, for example, a judge consider as valid, simply for reasons of legal security, the assignation of an unjust punishment or crime which happened to accord with this principle?

---

11 K. LARENZ: *Methodenlehre der Rechtswissenschaft*, Berlin/Heidelberg/New York (Springer) 4th ed. 1979, p. 68.

12 "The law cannot generate an interpretation of itself" (A. ROSS: *Theorie der Rechtsquellen*, 1929). "No one can overcome this maxim" (K. ADOMEIT: *Normlogik-Methodenlehre-Rechtspolitologie. Gesammelte Beiträge zur Rechtstheorie 1970-1985*, Berlin (Duncker Humblot) 1986, p. 201).

13 A definition of the law was given by article 590 of the USSR Penal Code: "The law is a system of social relationships serving the interests of the ruling classes and therefore protected by the power which they have organized, i.e. by the state", in: L. SCHMIDT (Ed.): *Schlagfertige Definitionen von Aberglaube bis Zynismus*, Hamburg (Rororo) 1987, p. 191.

Article 138 of the Turkish Constitution states that judges act independently and charges them with making decisions according to their conscience in light of the constitution and the law. Close scrutiny reveals that this article will not be of much help in answering our question. If the concept of the law here must be taken, not as the universal idea and culture of law but rather as the legal order of a country, then it allows very little leeway for creativity in handing down judgement, for the judge is instructed to make even his or her decisions of conscience conform to this framework.[14] The judge is then, in an Austinian sense,[15] still the servant of those who rule.

In face of the argument of injustice (*das Unrechtsargument*)[16] encompassed by our first question above, the German Higher Courts adopt the famous formula of Radbruch to lend judges important ethical support.[17] The formula runs as follows: "The conflict between justice and security of the law can be resolved by according priority to positive law, even if the latter, secured through legislation and governance, is unjust and inappropriate in content, only provided that the conflict between a positive code and justice becomes so intolerable that the code, as 'wrong law', must retreat a step in the face of justice".[18]

As in the postulate of the independent, neutral judge, this criterion too implies philosopher judges[19] who, in the words of Tevfik Fikret, are "free in

---

14 Article 132 of the 1961 Consititution states that "Judges shall make their decisions in accordance with the Constitution, the law and their conscience", a formulation which appears to allow the judge more creativity.

15 See A. GÜRIZ, *Hukuk Felsefesi*, Ankara (Ankara University, Faculty of Law Publ.) 1985, p. 313 ff.; J. AUSTIN: *Lectures on Jurisprudence II*, London (Campbell) 4th ed. 1873.

16 Concerning the argument of injustice see R. ALEXY: *Begriff und Geltung des Rechts*, Freiburg/Br, München (Karl Alber) 1992, p. 52 ff., R. DREIER: *op. cit.*, p. 99 ff.

17 BVerfGE 3, 58 (119); 3, 225 (233); 6, 132 (198); 6, 309 (332); 6, 389 (414 f.) 54, 53 (67 f.); BGHZ 3, 94 (107); 23, 175 (181); BGHSt 2, 173 (177); 2, 234 (238 f.); 3, 357 (362 f.); R. ALEXY: *op. cit.*, p. 53.

18 G. RADBRUCH: "Gesetzliches Unrecht und Übergesetzliches Recht", in: E. WOLF and H.-P. SCHNEIDER (Eds.): G. RADBRUCH: *Rechtsphilosophie*, Stuttgart (K.F. Köhler) 8th ed. 1973, p. 343 ff. See also H. ÖKÇESIZ: *Sivil Itaatsizlik*, *op. cit.*, p. 131ff.

19 H. ÖKÇESIZ: "Özgür Düşünmenin Hukuk ve Devlet Felsefesi", in: H. ÖKÇESIZ (Ed.): *Düşünce Özgürlüğü*, Istanbul (AFA) 1998, p. 123; Comp. AHMET

mind, in conscience and in understanding". Like the "civil servant scientist", the "civil servant judge" is awkwardly situated, for dedication to the truth and justice is incompatible with service to the power of government. If justice is the basis of the state —*iustitia fundamentum regnorum*—, then it is an utter contradiction to reverse the proposition, specifying the values that underly justice, and then put forward the same thesis. If justice is the basis of the state, then the state (government, the public good, national sovereignty, democracy, etc.) cannot be the foundation of justice.

The judge has power to dictate the use of force vis-à-vis the lives and property of others, but his "freedom" (as mentioned above) does not pose a threat to persons, rather being a vehicle of their protection. Law in society is a fact oriented toward the values of justice[20]; and if law for the individual means seeking justice[21] while justice means *neminem laedere*[22] —inflicting harm on no one— and doing that which does not harm others is freedom[23], then the judge should have the authority to know and to judge, an authority which he can place in this framework, and which in all its details will reflect a principle which renders meaningful the idea of the rule of law: *in dubio pro libertate* (when in doubt, rule in favor of freedom). This implies above all that there will be no shrinking, through some fear of arbitrariness, from the responsibility for freedom devolving on the judge. And the judge cannot transfer to another that which he does not have within himself. Furthermore, arbitrariness is not the result of freedom but of irresponsibility, inexperience, fear, repression and violence. An attempt to apply the law blindly and slavishly; a passive, uncritical adherence to models such as "the letter of the law", "the prevailing view in case law", or the unwritten general criteria of conformity, are in fact nothing more than a retreat into the deceptive ease of irresponsibility while hiding behind a shield of anonymity.

AKGÜNDÜZ: *Mukayeseli Islam ve Osmanlı Hukuku Külliyatı*, Diyarbakır 1986, p. 764.

20 G. RADBRUCH: *op. cit.*, p. 119.

21 G. RADBRUCH: *op. cit.* p. 327.

22 *Iuris praecepta sint haec: honeste vivere, alterum non laedere, suum cuique tribuere* – The three precepts of law are to live honorably, not harm others, and give to each as is his due. *Digesta* 1, 1, 10: 1 (Pseudo-Ulpian), *Lateinische Rechtsregeln und Rechtssprichwörter*, translated and edited by D. LIEBS, Darmstadt (WBG) 1982, p. 104.

23 "Freedom is being able to do all that which does not harm others", Article 4 of the 1789 French Declaration on Human and Citizen's Rights.

The judge cannot, however, shirk his or her responsibility of knowing the law, nor the freedom to seek and know which this necessitates. In the fashioning and creation of the law —*ius est ars boni et aeque* (law is the art of equity and justice.)[24]— the judge cannot underestimate his or her own primary role. Parliament makes laws, but the judge makes the law. "Judge" here is at first in the singular. *Summum ius summa iniuria* (Excess in applying laws can be a great injustice.)[25] is at times another way of expressing the admonition against the arbitrariness which arises from conformity.

I would at this point like to offer certain results from an unpublished empirical study which embraces a question that arises within the framework of the argument of injustice mentioned above. The study, based on a poll taken in late June of 1994[26], was designed to generate data and conclusions which might help in measuring "How Court of Appeals Judges See the Rule of Law". At that time there were a total of 637 members of the Court of Appeals: 80 prosecutors, 231 department heads and members, and 326 investigative judges. Through a jurist having the status of Court of Appeals assistant secretary and investigative judge we distributed 585 questionnaires, the responses being collected in the space of about a month. Questions 1-10 were devoted to matters of a social nature, 11-16 to professional position and areas of activity, 17-24 to political views, and 25-27 to the subjects' concept of the rule of law. 149 questionnaires were returned to us, 436 eliciting no response, and only 40 were answered in full, i.e. 109 were returned blank. Thus the actual response rate was some 7%. Chiefly responsible for this low figure is the well-known reticence of the courts. If we were able to evaluate certain answers, it is largely because the Appeals Court judges displayed a homogeneity in regard to certain questions, a conformity and consistency in group terms.

The question which concerns us here was framed as follows: "Would you deem it legitimate for a judge to seek to transcend a legal norm which he or she found egregiously injust?" (question 23). 23 respondents answered yes, and 17 no, a 57.5% affirmative result which indicates that judges avoid an

---

24 *Digesta*, 1,1, 2.

25 CICERO, *De Officiis*, 1-33.

26 The poll was carried out by myself in collaboration with Prof. Dr. Ülker Gürkan, a faculty member in the Ankara University Faculty of Law, Department of the Philosophy and Sociology of Law, together with Ahmet Haluk Atalay, research assistant in Marmara University Faculty of Law.

irresponsibly rigid positivism or extremely conceptualist approach to the law, that in case of egregious injustice they could give security of the law secondary consideration if it conflicted with justice, and that in the interaction between legal norms and social reality they were concerned that there be no perception of unfairness.

This result may imply the image of a judge trained in the development shown by the modern idea of the rule of law in its legal-methodological aspect, and in the issues which that modern idea has raised.

IV. The Touchstone of Judgement: Freedom of Expression, the Death Penalty and Civil Disobedience

While invoking both class and political concepts of judgement in pointing to the utopian aspect of the judge as neutral and independent third party, it behooves us at the same time to acknowledge that both these concepts are closely related to the transformation in legal methodology observable in the development of the rule of law.[27]

On certain planes, judgement is a class and political phenomenon, as borne out by innumerable observations. When their turn comes round, the judged become the judgers to enact political judgement. That being the case, political judgement, whatever its degree or the form it takes, must be humanized by the judge. Examination of the concepts of justice that have been handed down in human societies reveals that the role of judge has been defined by various codes: one may cite such principles as the casting of the first stone; loathing not the sinner but the sin; that mutual obligations apply

27 "... Thanks to this distinct legal path, the downtrodden class may find some advantage in the implementation of the law established by the ruling class. Thus in various struggles engaged in on behalf of the law by the downtrodden class, the latter becomes the guardian of a legal order imposed upon it by the ruling class. For, class law though it may be, it is still law, expressing the interests of the ruling class not overtly, but in the guise of law. Whatever the content of the law may be, the fact of legal form serves the downtrodden" (G. RADBRUCH, "Hukuk Devleti", trans. into Turkish by H. ÖKÇESIZ, *Argumentum*, 1 (1990), p. 16.)

to mortals, not to God; that justice has supreme priority; that the judge occupies the seat of the prophet; and that man is made in the image of God.

Once having said that social life gains continuity not through conflict but through compromise, if follows that the postulate of the neutral, independent judge must be supplemented by universal legal principles conveying both content and process. In our age the idea of law embraced by the rule of law has crystallized to a point which allows the judge such vast powers. The humanizing by the judge of everyday political jurisdiction is then achievable if the two-and-a-half millennia of knowledge and wisdom contained in legal ethics are transformed into the judge's individual professional conscience and become embodied in his or her legal deliberations.

The judge under today's rule of law faces three distinct tests, related with utmost directness to political judgement: in the name of taking legislative measures and attaining certain objectives, the expression of some ideas is at times prohibited, and the death penalty imposed for certain crimes. Meanwhile acts of civil disobedience quite different in nature from terrorism and anarchy are at times carried out. While inherently illegal, these acts raise an issue of ethical legitimacy which confronts us on the plane of human dignity, the debate over crimes of conviction and the death penalty.

If the rule of law and law itself are to be placed on a humane footing, the concept of human dignity must constantly be filled anew in terms of content. This, in turn, implies that it must be kept empty, and that is one benefit of a secular state. For ideal and real discourse to come about (J. Habermas – A. Kaufmann[28]) and be reflected in the judge's praxis, concepts of this type must at all costs avoid a dogmatic or ideological rigidity. For the true benefit of this concept lies in its remaining empty. As Lao Tse said, the emptiness of a pitcher is what makes it useful.[29] In humanizing political judgement, the judge updates the idea of human dignity which underlies the rule of law.

It behooves the judge, as it does every human individual, to ponder crimes of conviction, the death penalty and civil disobedience, and to act on the basis of his or her conclusions.

Given our legal system, however, the judge who finds that punishing crimes of conviction, or inflicting the death penalty, violates human dignity

28 A. KAUFMANN: *Hukuk Dogmatiği, Hukuk Kuramı*, trans. into Turkish by H. Ökçesiz, Istanbul (Alkım) 1993, pp. 18-20.

29 LAOTSE: *Tao Te King*, trans. by VICTOR VON STRAUSS, Zurich (Manesse) 1959, p. 68.

and therefore the rule of law, and who believes that civil disobedience should be dealt with separately from other offenses, finds him- or herself in a difficult position.

So placed, the judge has two choices. He or she can say: "I am opposed, but I will express my reservations publicly in writing and verbal statements, not permitting them to be reflected in my juridical activity". This approach is Kantian,[30] holding that the judge must not interpret a law but merely implement it. In this view the judge, like the soldier and priest, can express his or her views to the public only in an open use of reason (*der öffentliche Gebrauch der Vernunft*), and not while actually judging (*der Privatgebrauch der Vernunft*). The two are kept clearly separate, as the open or public use is encouraged by the enlightenment philosophy. In another approach, the judge applies, because of political pressure or the need to earn a livelihood, a law which offends his or her conscience, but reproaches the legislator and is aggrieved, his or her attitude being semi-passive. Here there is no question of spiritually active decision, autonomous in terms of conscience. Nor does this judge contemplate helping to overcoming this obstacle via a public use of reason. Such an application of the law is rooted primarily in fear and anxiety. Ultimately, if his or her power to create law or otherwise interpret it do not make it possible to overcome this contradiction, the judge will recognize that the underpinnings of legitimacy in approaches of either kind do not permit him or her adequately to retain an integrity of spirit and conscience;[31] that the responsibility entailed by the judicial function does not imply unconditional application of the law; and that this conflict, which is at the same time internal, cannot possibly be compensated. And he or she will see that no choice remains but to resign his or her post.

Where the freedom of the judge to create law is denied, this time bomb will explode either in his own conscience, or in his social role. Furthermore, where this freedom is denied, people will look for justice from those whom by the rules they are not called upon to trust; a situation which constitutes a widening, in society, of the wound opened in the judge's conscience.

---

30 I. KANT: "Beantwortung der Frage: Was ist Aufklärung?", in: W. WEISCHEDEL (Ed.): *Kant Werke in Zwölf Bänden XI*, Frankfurt/M (Suhrkamp) 1964, p. 57.

31 For this schematic of personal integrity (related to life, spirit and conscience), which in my view provides the content of the concept of human dignity, see H. ÖKÇESIZ, *Özgür Düşünmenin Hukuk ve Devlet Felsefesi*, *op. cit.* p. 40 ff.

If the legislative majority sees it as an undermining of the state order for the judge to make a contribution, using his or her free will, to what the legislature wills, then that state order can never be the rule of law; for the same so-called danger is amply implied by this free participation expected of the citizenry. Thus a legislative majority which denies judges the freedom to create law is in no position to desire freedom for others, whoever they may be.

The real problem, however, is the type of judge who, as (covertly) with the legislative majority attitude mentioned above, does not make human dignity the basis of his or her legal concerns, deliberations and actions. Such people are easy and inexpensive to crank out; current educational and training programs in the law, highly inadequate as they are, will produce more of these judges.

Chapter 10

Ethics and Politics

MÜMTAZ SOYSAL

It is not my intention here to discuss the various meanings of the word "ethics"; but at the outset I would like to make it clear —and perhaps this is the very aim of my talk— that I do not belong to the relativist school. Ethics should not be relative; and this is evident if one considers that ethics is not only the knowledge of a morality, but also the science of shaping morality and seeking what is right. However, as we all know, there are many ethics, a broad range. In order for one to be interested in such a branch of philosophy, these ethics must be essentially the same —apart from details— not only in different professions, but also in different countries and through all ages.

About three years ago, there was a series of talks on a similar topic, politics and morals or morality in politics. It was organized by our Faculty, the Ankara University Faculty of Political Science, and I took part in it by speaking of the ethical problem faced by those people we call politicians. We all exaggerate the difficulties of our own profession, and in that talk, in order to illustrate how hard my present profession is, I enumerated a whole array of difficulties. Of course for those with a relativistic outlook —among whom Machiavelli is sometimes mistakenly cited— politics is, to begin with, the most rampantly immoral field of endeavor on earth. As you know, however, Machiavelli did not strictly advocate immorality; yet that is the impression which has been given of him. Politics is known as a zone which, though it doesn't have to be immoral, is considered as being so. To those who view things in this light, it is difficult, specifically for a universty professor, to leave what he is doing and enter politics.

All of us have ethical problems in daily life, but they crop up far more often in politics. Needless to say, in solving these problems there are difficulties which by far transcend those encountered when person-to-person matters are involved. Some apply in all fields of endeavor; for example, one is not doing a job alone, but in conjunction with other people, collectively. It is done via party channels, in a party context, so an individual's own ethic must combine with others to become a collective ethic —and if it cannot, the attendant difficulties must be overcome by the individual. And in politics, one acts within a hierarchy. There are limits to what you can do on your own, and you are not the one to have drawn them. As has just been mentioned, there are regulations, laws, and even universal principles reflected in them.

And then there is something called party discipline, much less strict in many other professions than in politics, and less difficult. Military discipline is in a way harsh, but easy —you simply do your duty. In politics discipline is not such an easy matter, and I will return to this point later with greater emphasis. In politics, beyond speech and the development of ideas, there is action; for one strives to reach a position which permits action, and that is power. Politics without the idea of power is unthinkable, whether the idea of power within one's own organization, or the power of that organization vis-à-vis other organizations within the nation as a whole. But the thirst for it is a *sine qua non.* Why shouldn't we thirst for power? It's easy to criticize, easy to advise —but things are amiss in our country, and it is only those who hold power who can do something, act to stop them. That's why a giving up the thirst for power strikes me as alien to the concept of political party, and indeed to the concept of politics.

In politics your actions do not affect you alone, or your immediate circle or your party. In other professions this is only partially true. In every profession everybody wishes to rise in order to accomplish something; but politics means seeking power in order to direct the entire society. Without that power, your political aims cannot be reached.

Your actions in politics affect people in greatly varying ways. Let me give you the least dramatic example: if your country's foreign minister or deputy prime minister chases after the president of another country to shake his hand, if he or she can reconcile that attitude with his or her own ethics, this will be injurious to you as well, to sixty million people. It affects them, it aggrieves them; that is to say, in politics a very innocent act can touch the whole society, so that chasing someone at that moment is no longer a question of individual ethics. The assessment must be made taking into consideration what the whole society will say, not merely from the standpoint of relative ethics, but of universal ethics, considering, indeed, what humanity everywhere will say.

Particularly in our time, this aspect of the matter is becoming ever more salient; for there is a point which other professions do not share to the same degree: everything in politics happens for all to see, and this "all" does not mean just hundreds or thousands, but literally hundreds of millions of eyes. At least there is a stupendous communications web, incredibly extensive media, set up to make this so. Of course the media does not bring out the dramatic side of matters from a relative ethical standpoint, but indirectly forces one to think about events in absolute ethical, universal terms.

One thing which makes this political action more difficult —the political action for coming to power— is that because you are part of a collective movement you must explain what you do to others and convince them that you are right. Something done in accordance with your own ethical values must be adopted by a whole set of other people or else it cannot be translated into action. Whereas a judge has no such concerns. Indeed, if he is a real judge, indifferent to pressure from the outside, the verdict will be in strict accordance with the law and its norms, whether they derive from natural law or universally acknowledged texts, and there the problem ends; for even though that verdict may interest a large number of people, it is an individual one. Such is not the case in politics. To be effective, one's viewpoint must be adopted by others, encompassed by their ethics and indeed made part of their flesh and blood, or it cannot become a real political force.

This is perhaps not the place to bring up other contradictions encountered in politics, for I am not sure how much they fall under the heading of ethics. For example you may advocate, in line with your own convictions, that such and such be done in the country, for instance that, economically speaking, the government should encourage savings to be channeled into investment. But at the same time there's a national problem of unemployment. Available resources are limited, and you would like to solve the problem in a rational way, but let us assume that you have influence in certain industrial circles and that people force you to use this influence to place 200 workers in jobs which can be done by only one hundred, this situation conflicts with your ideas of productivity, savings, rationality and so on. Nevertheless such a step is proposed to you. Willy-nilly, you're forced to put people in those jobs. Why? Because if you don't, you'll be a bad politician. You'll lose votes in your constituency, they'll say "He didn't find jobs for our town", and you'll pay the price at the ballot-box. I'm not trying to create an ethical dilemma out of this, but politics may have that sort of dimension.

I. Philosophical Schools and Politics

In that same talk I ventured as well to speak of a defect common to the historians of philosophy. They constantly speak of thinkers and schools of thought, but without establishing the links between them. The connections over time that join human mind to the origins of thought, its progress and destiny, are not very well exposed.

What is the result? Well, people make their own connections, as I do —connections which seem appropriate to them, but which might amuse a philosopher. The mention of "ethics and politics", for example, makes me think of three widely divergent philosophers: Plato, Kant and Marx, who to some of you may appear totally unrelated.

In order to find, or formulate, a political ethics in my own mind, to ferret out what is right, it seems to me that there may be a connection linking these three. Of course at first glance Plato's is a very simple ethic, not terribly realistic today, one which might very crudely be summed up as follows: "If only philosophers could rule, society would be better". That is to say, if rulers were both virtuous and wise, loving virtue and wisdom, all society would benefit. So says Plato, but everyone realizes that this is very anti-democratic. Indeed, we would hold that it is anti-democratic not just by the standards of today, but even by those of Classical Greece. That classical view did not even consider elections democratic, and depended more on the drawing of lots. If society is going to govern itself by direct participation, but cannot gather all people in one place, then at least by the drawing of lots one can form a society in miniature —with proportionate numbers of the stupid, intelligent, virtuous and unvirtuous, and society will indeed be governing itself. If that is how we define democracy, as the governing of society by itself, then this is more democratic, and Plato's model is not very undemocratic at all.

But should it be rejected out of hand, even in our time? Should it be forgotten, discarded as being wrong —or is it not the duty of the politician, something he should do as part of, or in the course of, his business, to question the righteousness of action? Shouldn't he be concerned with the universality, or lack of it, in what people take for a "right action"?

Considered in this light, can't the politician be compared to a philosopher, or at least to a student of philosophy? For he may assess his actions in two different ways: 1. From the standpoint of personal success, he or she must ask: "Am I advancing? Is my party winning? Are we gathering votes?" And once these questions have been answered there comes another: "What is all this for? Is it for fame and glory, for money and the like, or, more consonant with how we define a politician, is it rather for accomplishing something?" If the object were to achieve something for himself, he would have become a businessman, and satisfied his ego in a myriad of ways. But seeing that he has chosen the field of politics, he has elected to do something for the society. And the moment he feels that it is necessary to act on behalf of the society, the concept of what is right comes into play. He must give satisfaction not merely as regards issues that are social, economic, and the like, but also to people *per se*, especially those who, whether soundly or ineptly, are in search of what is right. The devout, for example, with no thought for philosophy, believe in rectitude simply because, with their set of beliefs, they presume to know what is right and feel no need to know in any other way. I would hold that the politician senses better than any of us that this quest for the right is a shared one. In fact, sensing, feeling, intuiting, these do not run contrary to philosophy. Bergson built his philosophy on intuition. In face-to-face relationships it may not be so hard to guess what the other is thinking, but if, as in politics, you deal with millions of people on a day-to-day basis that skill of intuition must be highly developed. Some call it intuiting the "people's spirit", the "*Volkgeist*". Whatever, it is a necessary attribute in the politician. Just at present, for example, it is impossible for the politician not to sense that the society craves a bit more honesty, a bit more ethics, a bit more common sense and logic. If the politician doesn't sense this, he will go astray, and find himself at odds with the society. What's more, the politician must believe that this will be the fate of all those who so err. For this reason he may be best placed among all those who seek universality of this kind, not relativistically but in the sense of being able to partake in that unflagging quest of mankind for what is true and right. To do this, however —and here I return to Plato— he must not simply be versed in history, geography, law and so forth; he must also be steeped in the human sciences, and in philosophy, which is the science of thought. Sheer intuition will not do

—for when equipped with knowledge even intuition becomes more effective. That is why, to use a famous expression, I do not consign Plato to the dustbin of history.

Turning to Kant, we can most succinctly epitomize the basis of his philosophy by saying: "So act that the principles of your will may become a universal law".

The politician is a legislator, a maker of laws; and to make valid laws, laws which will be considered valid not only from the viewpoint of his own society, but also as viewed from without, he must first of all behave in a fashion which the law seeks to institutionalize, or he will lack credibility and persuasiveness. Fraud cannot produce a good law; or if it does, even when that law may seem good, people will not believe in it, or outside observers may say: "This law was made by a swindler, so probably something's up". Therefore the rule you wish to enshrine in law should be that which governs your own behavior. That is why I like Kantian ethics. It is far removed from relativism, and perhaps I am unable to express it in your terms; but it is a truth, an ethos, discovered by practical intelligence. It is for this reason I believe that Kant's ethics is still viable in our day. Without him, I feel that one may easily fall into relativistic ethics and be dragged into meaningless actions.

Why do I connect this with Marx? Actually, some say there is no such thing as Marxian ethics; for in his view all this is a reflection of the society's infrastructure. But precisely at that point there is, perhaps not an ethos, but an approach which might serve as a precept for political action: Why do people sometimes behave this way? Why do they rob and kill? Some explain it genetically and say: "They're born that way"; others, religions and the like, have their own explanations; but looking at the problem from Marx's standpoint one says: "because of economic and social conditions", concluding that these must be changed for the improvement of man's nature. How people can give up such a lofty ideal is incomprehensible, for it is truly an exalting, almost divine idea —an idea that competes with God. Some say that He created us this way, but I say: "No, we will be different, better". And to achieve this I propose to change certain economic and social conditions. In my opinion this has the potential of becoming a marvelous dynamo for human history; but it has been very badly applied. I won't go into the details of that, but rejecting the idea out of hand is utterly wrong.

MÜMTAZ SOYSAL

II. A New Dimension?

Looking at our own period (I do not call it an age), we see that in the last five or ten years the idea of changing societies —some drastically simplify the matter under the heading "voluntarism"—, this whole concept of altering the society, whether from above or below, is depicted as voluntarism or Jacobinism, and invites anger. Well, the idea of changing human nature by changing society has been pretty much discarded in our time.

Thank goodness this fashion is now somewhat fading, but up until a year or so ago an American theoretician was saying: "After trying various schools of philosophy, human thought has at last found what it was seeking. History is now at an end; or at least there is no longer much need to make the effort of thinking. We can be well satisfied with the present position of mankind: Democracy, human rights, and so on and so forth". Included in all this, as I tried to explain at another session of our Philosophical Society, has been the market economy, which in a highly peculiar manner has found its way into international texts. This was the subject of my talk on that occasion.[1] After the merging of East and West, it is in the Paris Charter, and its document on human rights, that we first see added to the triad of democracy, pluralism and human rights, a new concept: the market economy. Indeed, the latter is seen as inseparable from that triad. Yet if you go back 20 or 30 years, to the signing of the NATO pact, the nations who said they were coming together in the spirit of a philosophy based on those three principles —democracy, human rights and pluralism— put no such item in the preamble of the NATO pact. At that time it was nowhere to be seen, even though perhaps all of the societies concerned had essentially come into being through the development of a liberal economy. Yet they did not list this as the basic element or the underlying philosophy of their fundamental thought. That came later. The expectation that human nature can be changed is now at an end, although this is not said overtly. No one cares, in fact, whether mankind changes or not, because it is said that happiness has been found. If one ethical problem is the conflict between individual and social happiness, well, the solution to this has also been found; so it is now a matter of saying: "if

1 SOYSAL, M.: "Contradictions in the 'Human Dimension' of the Paris Charter", in: I. KUÇURADI (Ed.): *The Idea and the Documents of Human Rights*, Ankara (Philosophical Society of Turkey) 1995.

this can also enable people to be happy as individuals, then there is no problem for the society which encompasses them". Whereas even in our society and unquestionably in a major portion of the world, it is not clear whether this last element, the free market economy, will indeed give rise to that happiness and create the social order which democracy, universal human rights and pluralism are supposed to lead to, or whether in fact it will in many respects do the opposite.

In my mind, of course, the answer is clear. It will not do the job. For it will lead to harsher reaction. But in much of today's world great faith is placed in it.

Perhaps this is not the place for it, and perhaps some of our guests will be offended, but on the way here I saw an article by Herzinger in this week's *Die Zeit* criticising President Roman Herzog. Herzog had written a piece on human rights in the September 7, 1996 issue of the magazine in which he recognizes three types of human rights. But his is not the classic division into individual rights, economic-social rights and collective rights; nor as first and second generation of rights. No; Herzog first speaks of "fundamental rights". Most fundamental of all is the individual's right to life; the inviolability of the human body, the ban on torture etc., the right not to be subjected to inhumane actions and the ban on discrimination. Whatever the ethnic roots people may have, as human beings they should be considered within the same category. All this Herzog sees as "fundamental human rights". Then come the classic rights of the individual, where, he says, one must be tolerant. But then things become a bit confused. There are certain rights, he says, which in some countries are still at a developing stage, and if they do develop they will enable the first and second category rights to develop also —and therefore the violation of these latter can for the moment be tolerated to a degree. The rights which will accomplish this, which thus must be viewed positively, are those of property and free economy. The article I have just read is a reaction, and one point on which Herzinger takes umbrage is that, astonishingly, freedom of thought is grouped in neither the first nor the second category. Here, too, says Herzog, one must be tolerant —he goes so far as to maintain that, specifically to enable societies to achieve property rights, the free market and so forth, their relegation of this freedom to a back burner can be tolerated.

How can one possibly separate freedom of thought from the integrity of the body and the ban on torture? This is totally incomprehensible. Freedom of thought could easily take its place in the first category. From a political standpoint, if you take politics to mean not just seeking power to change things in one's own society, but in the broader sense of changing the world, then if every element affects the others, how much prosperity and happiness can you achieve for your own society without at least pursuing that ideal of world-wide change? That being the case, one must willy-nilly have a world vision. With the political philosophy we have just noted, its reflection in politics, the reflection of such distinctions, and such a value system, might be as follows: one can put up with certain things in certain societies, even though they do not adhere completely to universal norms. But if they are indeed basic, fundamental rights, then in that first category —the right to life, the integrity of the body, the ban on torture, non-discrimination— any violation is intolerable. But unless you include freedom of thought under this heading, the basis of your other tolerance is weakened. For if a society has essentially succeeded in these universal matters, you may overlook its failure to completely guarantee the other rights, adopting the attitude of a teacher who sees improvement and trusts that eventually the "student" will pass. But if that society has failed to embrace the freedom of thought as an inviolable right, then there is no promising beginning about which to be charitable. In his article, on the eve of the president's visit to Iran and China, Herzinger says he feels compelled to note this, and he therefore maintains that Iran can be viewed with slightly greater tolerance.

III. Freedom of Thought as the Foundation of Politics

But here one faces a very different beginning. This is why I hold that this category of basic rights is important. If the world and humanity at large are going to view with tolerance a society like ours where other rights are not yet well established —indeed, if that society is to tolerate itself—, these fundamental rights must be unquestionably in place for the start to be deemed a good one. In other words, that starting point allows of no compromise. If you say: "We are against discrimination, but we have to practice it a bit —we view some people as more worthy than others"; or "We respect human life and the integrity of the body, but now and then the police have to twist a few arms", that is a compromise which should not be made. You have a political ethic and believe that it should be universal, then in these matters there can be no compromise, no bargaining, no concession. These matters are fundamental. Respect for man and respect for the human body mean non-discrimination as to race, language, religion and the like, plus —and I find it incomprehensible to leave this out— respect for freedom of thought, the one element among all others which makes us human beings. Without freedom of thought, what is gained by protecting the integrity of the body and so forth? One does not deprive people of their humanity by dragging them on the ground or jolting them with electricity; but if you deny them the right to think and speak out, obstructing the thing which most makes them human, then indeed you rob them of humanity. That is why on this matter there can be no compromise —the freedom must be absolute.

But in our country, and some of you have experienced this personally, the belief I have outlined is still lacking. When that is the case, just as when people are denied the right to live or deprived of their humanity, there is no meaning in the claim that one pursues such and such an ideal to create a happy society. When people cannot express their views it will at any rate be difficult to achieve that happiness; for if the poor cannot speak of their poverty, if misery cannot be spoken, if complaints are not expressed nor ideas openly set forth, then even the most tangible benefits cannot be obtained. For this reason freedom of thought plays a vital role in securing other rights.

Of course I am saying all this with something in mind: Politics is generally characterized with a word that in Turkish means "contemptible" or "sleazy". People ask things like "Why did you get into the sleaze of politics"? Whereas politics is perhaps exactly the reverse, a place of washing —washing in the sea of one's own society. And in the course of this washing, one becomes as purged as possible from all that runs counter to universality. When politics is pursued in this spirit, it brings relief not only to oneself but to society at large; although it may not always bring success. When viewed from the standpoint of success and failure, when measured by the criteria which this implies, one may seem, to some, to have failed. But perhaps the key to his success is the very absence of it. His failure may be success; if he can manage this cleansing, then he may be able to make both himself and his society happy, or at least those in it who are aware of the process. In this regard I can quite frankly say that I am not at all unhappy in politics.

List of Authors

KRITON CURI†, Professor of Civil Engineering, Boğaziçi University, Istanbul, Turkey.

ZEYNEP DAVRAN, Professor of Philosophy, Boğaziçi University, Istanbul, Turkey.

VITTORIO HÖSLE, Director, Hannover Institute of Philosophy, Hannover and Professor of Philosophy, Essen University, Essen, Germany.

PETER KOSLOWSKI, Director, Hannover Institute of Philosophy, Hannover and Professor of Philosophy and Political Economy, University of Witten Herdecke; Director of the Centre for Ethical Economics and Economic Culture of the Hannover Institute for Philosophical Research.

IOANNA KUÇURADI, Professor of Philosophy, Head of the Department of Philosophy and Director of the Centre for Research and Application of the Philosophy of Human Rights, Hacettepe University, Ankara, Turkey; President of the International Federation of Philosophical Societies.

FRIEDRICH KÜBLER, Professor of Civil Law, University of Frankfurt, Germany and University of Pennsylvania, USA.

KLAUS M. LEISINGER, Executive Director and Delegate of the Board of Trustees of Novartis Foundation for Sustainable Development and Professor of Development Sociology, Basel University, Switzerland.

HAYRETTIN ÖKÇESIZ, Associate Professor of the Philosophy and Sociology of Law, Marmara University, Istanbul, Turkey.

YAMAN ÖRS, Professor of Medical Ethics and Medical History, Ankara University, Turkey.

MÜMTAZ SOYSAL, Professor of Constitutional Law, Member of the Parliament, Ankara, Turkey.

HARUN TEPE, Associate Professor of Philosophy, Hacettepe University, Ankara, Turkey.

Index of Names

Page numbers in italics refer to quotations in footnotes or references

INDEX OF NAMES

INDEX OF NAMES

FSC
www.fsc.org
MIX
Papier aus verantwortungsvollen Quellen
Paper from responsible sources
FSC® C105338

If you have any concerns about our products,
you can contact us on
ProductSafety@springernature.com

In case Publisher is established outside the EU,
the EU authorized representative is:
Springer Nature Customer Service Center GmbH
Europaplatz 3, 69115 Heidelberg, Germany

Printed by Libri Plureos GmbH
in Hamburg, Germany